Art in Action

Credits

Cover: Illustration by Judy Sakaguchi.

Illustrations: 27(r), 61(r), 74(b), 75, 93(l), 113(r), 117(r), Barbara Hoopes; 121, Bernie Lansky; 123(r), Jeff Jurich.

Publisher's Photos: All photos by Rodney Jones Studios except as credited below. Key: (t) top, (c) center, (b) bottom, (l) left, (r) right.

UNIT 1: Page 3(r), Claude Haycraft/Camerique; 5(c), Lee Hanson; 9(l), Carl Purcell/Words and Pictures; 10(r), 15(l), Lee Hanson; 15(r), Leven Leatherbury; 16(r), Derek Fell; 18(l), E.R. Degginger; 22(l), Allen F. Grazer/The Stock Solution; 22(r), Courtesy of The New York Historical Society, New York; 23(l), 23(r), Lee Snider/Photo Images; 24, Ezra Stoller/Esto; 25(l), Otto B. Rigan; 27(l), Leven Leatherbury; 28(l), Bruce D. Thomas; 28(r), Ronald F. Ruhoff/Stock Imagery; 31, Geoffrey Clements.

UNIT 2: Page 34, Melvin L. Prueitt, IS-2, Los Alamos National Laboratory, author of *Art and the Computer,* McGraw-Hill, 1984; 37(l), 37(r), Lee Hanson; 42(tl), 42(br), John Tennant; 47(r), 49(l), Lee Hanson; 55(l), Sandak, Inc.; 56(l), Universal Studios; 59(l), Paul Cline; 59(r), Leven Leatherbury; 60(l), H.S. Rice; 63(l), Library of Congress; 63(r), Leven Leatherbury; 66, John Tennant; 68, Lee Hanson.

UNIT 3: Page 71(b), Norma Morrison; 72(t), Robert Capa/Magnum Photos, Inc.; 73, Muldoon Studio, Waltham; 76, Cleveland Metroparks Zoo, photo by Emily A. Votruba; 79(l), Geoffrey Clements; 79(r), David Schalliol; 81(l), Geoffrey Clements; 83(r), Lee Hanson; 84, Jerry L. Thompson; 85(tr), 85(br), Leven Leatherbury; 88(l), Lee Hanson; 88(r), Lorenza Fong; 89(l), Yale Athletics; 89(r), Lee Hanson; 92(l), 92(r), Lee Boltin; 93(c), 93(r), Leven Leatherbury; 94, 95(r), Lee Boltin; 96(r), Otto Nelson; 97(tl), 97(bl), Lee Hanson; 97(r), Hillel Burger; 99(l), Art Resource, NY; 100(t), Rick Oyama; 101, David Heald.

UNIT 4: Page 103(t), Elliott Varner Smith; 103(br), Lee Hanson; 104, Terry Heffernan/Light Language; 105(l), Lee Boltin; 106, Geoffrey Clements; 109(r), Lee Hanson; 112(r), DRK Photo; 113(l), Stephen Hilson/Alaska Photo; 115(r), Lee Hanson; 118(l), Bobby Hanson; 118(r), Geoffrey Clements; 125(r), Myles E. Baker; 128(l), 128(r), Don Miller; 129(l) Michael Alexander; 130(l), Geoffrey Clements; 130(r), Roberto Marchiori; 132(l), 132(r), 133(l), 133(r), Joel Hagen; 134, Leven Leatherbury.

Art in Action

Guy Hubbard

Indiana University

Contributing Educators:

D. Sydney Brown
Lee C. Hanson
Barbara Herberholz

CORONADO PUBLISHERS

San Diego   Orlando   Dallas   Chicago

Printed in the United States of America   ISBN 0-15-770052-6(5)

1 2 3 4 5 6 7 8 9 0 93 92 91 90 89 88 87

Table of Contents

Unit 1

Discovering Art Around You

Claude Monet, Sunflowers. 1881. Oil on canvas. 39¾" × 32". The Metropolitan Museum of Art, Bequest of Mrs. H.O. Havemeyer, 1929. The H.O. Havemeyer Collection.

Richard Estes, Helene's Florist. 1971. Oil on canvas. 48" × 72". The Toledo Museum of Art, Toledo, Ohio. Gift of Edward Drummond Libbey.

Many of the things you do in life had to be studied and learned. Other things may have seemed to come naturally, with little effort. Have you ever thought of *seeing* as something that you had to learn to do? Artists spend their lifetimes learning how to truly see all the wonder and beauty that exists in the world around them.

Art begins with observation. Art is discovery, a way of looking at the world as though you were seeing it for the first time. Not everyone will create works of art. But everyone can learn to see as an artist sees. Everyone can find and respond to the **elements of design** that fill our world with wonder: the **lines**, **shapes**, **forms**, **spaces**, **textures**, **values**, and **colors** that add interest and beauty to natural and man-made environments.

What do the two works of art shown here have in common? The first is a painting by a famous French artist of the nineteenth century. The second is a painting that looks like a photograph. It was painted by a **contemporary** American artist. Each work was created by a very different kind of artist, with a very different way of looking at the world. Yet, from flowers to flower shop, each artist saw something in the everyday environment that was worth expressing in a work of art.

Art is more than drawing, painting, sculpture, or photography. It is a way of seeing. Art is a great adventure, an experience in finding meaning in even common, ordinary things. As you learn to see the way an artist sees, you will understand that art is truly everywhere.

1

1 Artists Are Observers

Observing and Thinking

If you were asked to draw a picture of your home, could you remember what it looks like? Would you be able to draw its shape, the number of windows it has, or even the color of its outside walls?

When you have to draw something from memory without looking at the actual object, you must rely on your **visual memory**. Visual memory is an important skill for any artist to have. In order to develop a good visual memory, though, you have to learn to truly observe your environment.

Artists must train themselves to be careful observers of the things around them. Nothing is too small, too simple, or too common to be worthy of their attention. They draw, paint, sculpt, photograph, and make other works of art based on what they see in their world. Albrecht Dürer, one of the greatest artists of the **Renaissance**, drew and painted many objects from his daily life. His painting, *The Large Piece of Turf*, is one of his best-known works, and yet its subject is very ordinary: a clump of grasses and plants. What do you think Dürer saw in this simple subject that made him want to paint it?

Albrecht Dürer, The Large Piece of Turf. Albertina Museum, Vienna.

Leonardo da Vinci, Star of Bethlehem and Other Plants. *Reproduced by gracious permission of Her Majesty Queen Elizabeth II.*

Creating Art

1. Gather a collection of small natural and man-made objects that you find in your home, at school, and in various parts of your neighborhood.

2. Put your collected objects into a brown paper bag and bring them to class with you. Reach into the bag and choose an object to draw. Put it back into the bag without taking time to really study it. Now take a piece of drawing paper and fold it in half, as though you were making a greeting card. On the outside half of the paper, draw your object from memory. Try to remember what it looks like, and draw it as well as you can.

3. Remove the object that you drew from the bag. Carefully look at your object; feel its **texture** and observe its **shape**. Open up your paper and draw your object again. Keep looking at your object while you draw. Draw the main shape first, then add the details you can see. Use the sides of your pencil as well as the point. Make many different kinds of **lines** to show your object as it really appears.

4. Compare the two drawings that you made. Which one looks more like the actual object? If you drew the object again from memory, would it look more convincing than your first drawing?

Art Materials

Collection of found objects (pinecones, leaves, bits of machinery, seashells, etc.)	Brown paper sack White drawing paper Pencil

---

Learning Outcomes

1. Why must artists carefully study objects in their environment before they can successfully draw or paint them?

2. Which of your two drawings looked more like the object you were drawing? Why do you think so?

3. What interests you about the Dürer painting? Would you choose to paint such a simple subject?

3

2 Seeing Lines and Outlines

Observing and Thinking

Lines are part of most of the things we see around us. Can you think of some examples of lines in your everyday environment?

As you thought about all the kinds of lines you have seen, did it occur to you what a variety of lines there are? Some lines are straight, and some are curved; some lines are long, and some are short; some lines are thick, and some are thin. Lines **vary** in their length, width, direction, color, and even in the way they curve (or don't curve). Lines that have a particular path or movement, called **rhythm**, can have special names, such as zigzag, spiral, or wavy lines. Can you think of others?

When a line comes back around to meet itself at its starting point, it becomes a **shape**. A shape can be exact and **geometric**, such as a square, a triangle, or a circle. Shapes can also be **free-form**, made up of curving, irregular lines. The line that forms the edges of either kind of shape is called the **outline**, or **contour**.

Observe the kinds of lines used in the artworks shown here. How are they alike and different? Can you spot geometric or free-form shapes? What kinds of lines do you see in each work? Which work has a clear outline, or contour, that you can see?

Morris Graves, Bird in Spirit. Gouache on paper. 20″ × 30″.
The Metropolitan Museum of Art, The Arthur Hoppock Hearn Fund, 1950.

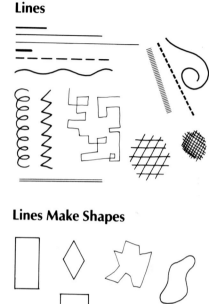

(Attributed to) Torii Kiyonobu I.
(1664–1729), A Woman Dancer. 21¾" × 11½".
The Metropolitan Museum of Art,
Harris Brisbane Dick Fund, 1949.

Lines

Lines Make Shapes

Creating Art

1. Use your visual memory or look at photographs to help you draw several pictures about the topic, "at the zoo." Use a variety of lines and shapes in your drawings. Choose the drawing you like best.

2. As your teacher directs, redraw your favorite picture on a flat piece of Styrofoam. Keep the drawing simple, and large enough to fill the Styrofoam surface. Make deep lines in the Styrofoam. You may need to go over your lines again and again so that they are deep enough.

3. Use a **brayer** to roll paint or printing ink all over the surface of the Styrofoam drawing. Then place a piece of paper on top of the inked drawing. Rub the back of the paper gently with your fingers or a spoon so that the paper picks up the image.

4. Carefully lift the paper off the Styrofoam block. You will have a colored print of your drawing, which you can sign and number.

Art Materials	
Smooth piece of Styrofoam	Lightweight paper
Pencil	Brayer and pan
Drawing paper	
Newspapers	Printing ink

Learning Outcomes

1. Name four ways that lines can vary.

2. What kinds of lines and shapes did you use in your zoo drawing?

3. Of the examples shown here, which artwork shows the greatest variety of lines?

3 Keep It Simple

Observing and Thinking

Do you remember when you first began to learn cursive handwriting? You may have found that it was somewhat like drawing. You made rounded, curving lines that flowed with **rhythm** and movement across a page.

A special form of handwriting is called **calligraphy**. Calligraphy is the art of beautiful lettering. You may have seen examples of this kind of fancy handwriting on greeting cards, posters, and wedding invitations. Certain drawings, made with a pen or brush, have some of the qualities of calligraphy. When a drawing is made up of flowing lines and shapes that are like those used in handwriting, we say that the drawing is **calligraphic**.

In the nineteenth century, some American schoolteachers and penmanship students used their handwriting skills to make calligraphic drawings. These artists drew simple animal shapes and pictures that told about America. The charming lion shown below, by an unknown American artist, is an example of this kind of calligraphic drawing.

Other calligraphic drawings are based on Oriental art styles. Picasso's *The Deer,* drawn with ink and brush, is influenced by a kind of Japanese brush drawing called **sumi-e**. John B. Flannagan's racing dog uses the Oriental qualities of simple curving lines to express shape and movement.

In calligraphic drawings, artists simplify the forms they draw. They use lines in an **expressive** way to show only what is most important in the subject they have chosen.

Young Lion. *Pen and brown ink on board. 18" x 24". M. and M. Karolik Collection of American Watercolors and Drawings, 1800-1865. Courtesy, Museum of Fine Arts, Boston.*

Pablo Picasso, The Deer. 1936, Aquatint. Printed in color. Composition: 10½" × 8¼". Collection, the Museum of Modern Art, New York. Gift of Abby Aldrich Rockefeller.

John R. Flannagan. Whippet. Crayon on paper. 10⅛" × 13⅞". The Seattle Art Museum, Eugene Fuller Memorial Collection. 39.48

Creating Art

1. Think of a subject that you could draw using flowing, rhythmic lines. You might decide to draw an animal, a place you know well, or a person.

2. Learn what kinds of lines you can make with a brush. Dip your brush in black paint or ink and practice making various kinds of lines on a piece of newsprint. Try painting with a nearly dry brush. What effect do you get? Now try painting with a wet brush. How are the two kinds of lines different? Pretend that you are handwriting with your brush. Make rounded, curving lines across your paper.

3. Begin your brush drawing on a clean sheet of paper. Do not draw your subject in pencil first. Instead, try to feel the movement of your subject. Show that movement with curving, rounded lines. **Vary** the

thicknesses of the lines you make. Remember, you are trying to draw only what is most important about your subject. Keep it simple!

Art Materials	
Brush and water container	Newsprint
Black paint or ink	White drawing paper

Learning Outcomes

1. What is calligraphy? What is a calligraphic drawing?

2. How did you keep your subject simple? What kinds of lines did you use?

3. Which of the three artists' drawings do you like best? Which one seems most like a calligraphic drawing to you? Why?

4 Creative Rubbings

Observing and Thinking

Have you ever placed a coin beneath a sheet of paper and rubbed a pencil over it to make a **rubbing**? Making rubbings from **raised surfaces** is a good way to learn about **textures**. It is possible to make rubbings from textured surfaces in nature, such as tree bark, as well as from man-made surfaces, such as manhole covers. Can you think of other textured surfaces in your environment from which rubbings could be made?

American artist Robert Indiana made the rubbing shown below. Indiana was a member of a group of artists of the late 1950s and early 1960s who called themselves **Pop artists**, because they used popular **contemporary** images as subject matter. They got their ideas from movies, comic books, and consumer products. Why do you think that a Pop artist would consider a rubbing a work of art?

Compare Indiana's rubbing with the **medieval** rubbing shown on the next page. What does each rubbing reveal about its time? What kind of image would you choose to represent the world we live in today?

Robert Indiana, The American Hay Company. 1962. Frottage in conté crayon. 25⅛″ × 19⅛″. Collection, The Museum of Modern Art, New York. Eugene and Claire Thaw Fund.

8

Creating Art

1. Sketch a design that represents something about you. Your design can show an object or an idea. You may include words as part of the design. Perhaps you would like to create your own plaque or manhole cover. Use simple shapes to make your design.

2. Draw your design on a piece of tagboard or thin cardboard. Cut out the pieces. Paste them on a sheet of paper or tagboard to recreate your design. These pieces will form a raised surface. You can build up your raised surface with two or more layers of pieces.

3. When the pieces are dry, place a thin sheet of paper over your design. Using the side of a peeled crayon or oil pastel stick, rub over and over the paper. Your design will show through the paper as a rubbing. You may wish to use more than one color to make your rubbing.

4. Many artists, including Robert Indiana, give their artwork a title. Think of a title for your rubbing and write it in the lower right-hand corner of the paper.

Art Materials	THINK SAFETY
Tagboard, thin cardboard, or old file folders	Thin paper
	Peeled crayons or oil pastels
Scissors	Pencil
Paste	Drawing paper

Learning Outcomes

1. What kind of subject matter did Pop artists use in their work?

2. How did you create a design that represents you?

3. Which objects in your community would make good sources for rubbings?

5 Learning to See a Tree

Observing and Thinking

When you were very young, did you draw trees that looked like lollipops? Such figures are more like **symbols** of trees than realistic drawings. If you look carefully at trees, you will see that they come in many **shapes**. Sometimes artists will simplify these shapes to make **abstract** drawings of trees. We can still recognize the tree shapes, but they do not look like the trees we see around us.

Look at a real tree. Observe the entire tree carefully. What is its main shape? Does it appear to be oval, square, rectangular, triangular, or even circular? What are the main shapes of the trees in the painting by Charles Burchfield shown on this page?

Now observe the trunk and branches of a tree. Can you find a place where the trunk has divided into branches? Do you see how the branches divide into even smaller branches? This is a good example of **progressive rhythm**. In progressive rhythm, bigger or wider parts of a thing continue to divide into smaller or narrower parts. Use your pencil to quickly sketch a branch, starting from the wide part and drawing out, and you will understand what is meant by this kind of rhythm.

Charles E. Burchfield, Hush Before the Storm. 1947. Watercolor on paper. 40″ × 30″. Courtesy Wichita Art Museum, the Roland P. Murdock Collection.

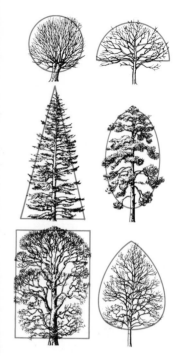

Tom Thomson, The Jack Pine/Le pin. *1916–17. Oil on canvas.*
127.9 × 139.8 cm. National Gallery of Canada, Ottawa.

Creating Art

1. Collect and study many photographs of trees. Also look at sketches of trees that you have made from life. Look for the main shapes and the rhythm of the parts of the trees. Use your photographs and sketches to make a drawing of a tree.

2. As you draw, be sure to show the bumpy edges of the tree's **outline**. Then show how the trunk divides into branches, and how the branches divide into smaller branches. Show this rhythm in your drawing, as though the tree were growing quickly before your eyes.

3. You may leave the branches bare, or you may draw in areas of leaves. Draw slowly and carefully, looking at photographs and your sketches as you draw.

4. Display your drawing with the other drawings your class has made. How many different shapes of trees are there?

Art Materials	
Drawing paper	Photographs and sketches of trees
Pencil	

Learning Outcomes

1. What are some of the things you look for when you draw a tree?

2. How did you make your tree look as realistic as possible?

3. Which of the two paintings shows main shapes and progressive rhythm best?

6 Shading and Adding Textures

Observing and Thinking

Do you think that a picture that isn't in color would be uninteresting? Some of the world's greatest photographs and drawings have been made in simple black and white. Do you see why Edward Weston's photograph of a pepper is considered a great work of art?

Edward Weston, Pepper No. 30, 1930. *Photograph. As published in* Edward Weston: The Flame of Recognition, *Aperture, New York City, 1965. © 1981 Arizona Board of Regents, Center for Creative Photography.*

In a black-and-white picture, colors show up as various **values**. Value means the lightness or darkness of an object. Between pure white and pure black there are hundreds of values of gray. Your own pencil can produce a wide range of values, from a light gray that is almost white to a dark gray that is almost

black. The illustration on page 13 shows the many values that you can make with a pencil, black crayon, or charcoal stick.

You can experiment with different values to produce **shading**. Shading is a way of making an object that you draw seem to be solid and **three-dimensional** rather than flat. In shading, you produce a very gradual change of values from light to dark to show light and shadows on an object. Shading is also a way to show the **texture** of an object. Lines and shading can show textures that are rough, smooth, coarse, or scratchy.

Thomas Cole, Gnarled Tree Trunk, c. 1826. Pen and brown ink over pencil. 14¹³/₁₆″ × 10¹¹/₁₆″. Detroit Institute of Arts. Founders Society Purchase, William H. Murphy Fund.

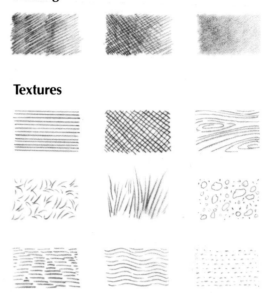

John Frederick Kensett, Birch Trees, Niagara. 1850. Pencil on paper. The Metropolitan Museum of Art, Morris K. Jessup Fund, 1976. (1976.19)

Shading

Textures

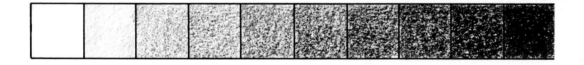

Creating Art

1. Experiment with making different values using the side of your pencil. See if you can make your own value scale, like the one in the illustration above. Also experiment with making different kinds of lines to show textures.

2. Study how the artists whose work is shown in this lesson used different values to show shading and texture in their drawings. Now, redraw the picture of the tree you drew in the previous lesson. This time, make it look more realistic by shading in light and dark parts. Try to show the three-dimensional **form** of the tree. Use different kinds of lines to indicate textures.

Art Materials

Drawing from previous lesson

Pencil or charcoal

White drawing paper

Learning Outcomes

1. Tell two things that shading can do to make a drawing look more realistic.

2. What kinds of lines did you use in your tree drawing to show texture?

3. Which of the tree drawings in this lesson shows the best use of shading and textures? Why do you think so?

7 A Colorful Crayon Etching

Observing and Thinking

At different times in your life, have you ever had a thought, feeling, or interest that meant a lot to you? Perhaps, at the time, it seemed to be the most important thing about you. Today, that important thing may not have the same meaning for you. It may not have the same **emphasis** (em'-fə-səs), or special importance, that it once had.

In every work of art, there is something that the artist feels is most important. He or she makes this part of the work the **center of interest**, or the point of emphasis. It may be a **shape**, a **form**, a **texture**, or another element of design that is emphasized in an artwork.

There are many ways to achieve emphasis in a work of art. Artists may use color, line, size, texture, shape, and the placement of objects to direct the observer's eye to the center of interest. In Paul Klee's *Fish Magic*, brilliant colors set against a dark background attract our eyes to the various parts of the picture. Lines also help move our eyes around the painting. In most works of art, there is one center of interest. Through skillful use of line and color, though, Klee has created more than one center of interest in this painting. Can you find these points of emphasis?

In this lesson, you will use color and line to make a **crayon etching** that shows how well you understand some ways to create a center of interest in art.

Paul Klee, Fish Magic. 1925. Oil on canvas mounted on board. 30⅜" × 38½". Philadelphia Museum of Art: Louise and Walter Arensberg Collection.

14

Creating Art

1. Completely coat a small sheet of white drawing paper with different light and bright crayon colors. You can make patches or bands of color. Press firmly with your crayons. Do not use dark colors.

2. When you have completely coated your paper with a solid layer of crayon colors, cover the top of your colored layer with black crayon. You will need to press very hard to make a black layer that covers the colored layer.

3. Choose a subject that has interesting lines and textures. You may want to draw an undersea world, as Paul Klee did. Draw your picture by etching, or scratching, it into the black layer of crayon. You can scratch out as much of the black as you wish. This will reveal the colors underneath. Keep scratching until you are satisfied with your picture. Try using all kinds of lines to create textures in your drawing. Do you see how the contrast of bright crayon colors against the black crayon creates emphasis in your picture? How else did you create a center of interest?

Art Materials	THINK SAFETY
Wax crayons	Drawing tools (paperclips, nails, etc.)
White drawing paper	
Newspapers	

Learning Outcomes

1. What is emphasis in a work of art? What are some things artists can do to create a center of interest?

2. What are some ways that crayon etching is different from other kinds of drawing you have tried?

3. What are some of the centers of interest in the painting by Paul Klee? Can you trace the lines that lead your eyes to these centers of interest?

8 The Colors of a Garden

Observing and Thinking

When you look at a flower garden, what colors do you see? A garden can be as colorful as an artist's paintbox, full of rainbow colors.

Artists must learn all they can about color so that they can use it effectively in their paintings. Painters soon learn that there are three colors they must have: red, yellow, and blue. These are the **primary colors**. Different combinations of these colors, or **hues**, make every other color, except white.

Two primary colors mixed together make a **secondary color**. Orange, green, and violet are the three secondary colors. Orange is made by mixing red and yellow together. What primary colors do you mix together to make green and violet?

The **intermediate colors** are "in-between" hues that come between the primary and secondary colors. Look at the names of these colors on the color wheel. How do you think these colors are made?

In this lesson, you will paint a garden, as many great artists have done. You will probably want to use these three kinds of colors you have learned about. Look at the painting by French artist Claude Monet. This painting is done mostly in primary and secondary colors. Are these the colors you would see in a garden? What kinds of colors do you see in the photograph of a garden, shown below? Could you mix these colors yourself?

Claude Monet, The Artist's Garden at Vetheuil. *The Norton Simon Foundation.*

16

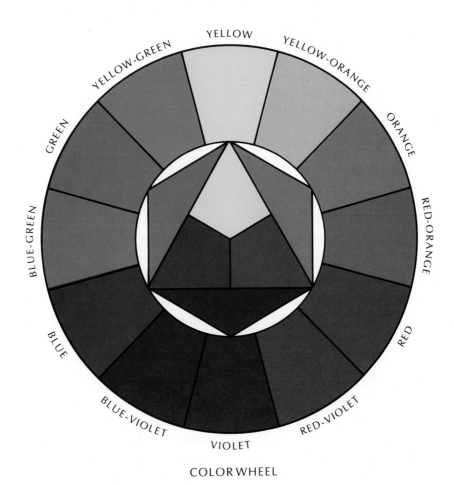

COLOR WHEEL

Creating Art

1. Practice mixing intermediate colors. Add varying amounts of a primary color to a secondary color and see what results you get. Use several sheets of paper for your experiments in color mixing.

2. When you feel confident about mixing colors, use your imagination to think of a garden you would like to paint. Your garden should be colorful and full of flowers. It does not have to look **realistic** or even use realistic colors. It should be your own special idea of a garden. Lightly **sketch** your garden scene first. Then paint it, using primary, secondary, and intermediate colors. Monet used blobs and swirls of color to make his painting of a garden. How did he show mood and feeling in his painting?

Art Materials	
Tempera paints	Brushes
Newsprint (for mixing experiments)	Water, paper towels
White drawing paper	Water container
Pencil	Mixing tray

Learning Outcomes

1. Name the primary, secondary, and intermediate colors. How do you make each type of color?

2. What colors did you use to paint your garden? Did you use color realistically?

3. How does Monet use color in his painting of a garden? In what ways can color be an important part of an artwork?

9 Selecting a View

Observing and Thinking

Do you ever take photographs with a camera? If you do, you know that you have to select what you want to photograph by looking through the little window in the camera called the **viewfinder**. The viewfinder shows you what will appear in the picture you're going to take. If you don't like what the viewfinder shows, you can move closer to or step back from the subject you are photographing. You can also decide what shape your picture will be. If you were photographing a tall building, for example, you would probably want to turn the camera so that the viewfinder shows a **vertical** picture. If you were looking at the Grand Canyon, you would probably want to take a **horizontal** picture. Why?

Artists who paint and draw also sometimes use viewfinders. An artist's viewfinder is a tool that helps the artist to focus on what is important in a scene. Pictures made without a real center of interest can be confusing to look at. With a viewfinder, an artist can choose to show the part of a scene that will make a good, interesting picture and block out other parts. Viewfinders help artists to **compose**, or decide what to include in, pictures that they create from life. Do you think that American artist John Sloan might have used a viewfinder to compose *The City from Greenwich Village*? Do you think that a horizontal shape is best for this **cityscape**, or view of a city?

John Sloan, The City from Greenwich Village. *1922. Canvas. 26″ × 33¾″.*
National Gallery of Art, Washington, D.C. Gift of Helen Farr Sloan.

Creating Art

1. First, fold a piece of thick paper in half. Cut a rectangular opening along the fold. When you open your paper, you will have a rectangular viewfinder.

2. Hold up your viewfinder in a vertical position. Look through it and see if you can find any scenes inside your classroom, outside the window, or on the playground with a definite center of interest. Try your viewfinder in a horizontal position, too. Which position is best for your view? When you find a view that you like, hold the viewfinder there.

3. Draw the scene you see. If you are holding your viewfinder in a vertical position, your paper should be vertical, too. Keep holding up your viewfinder. Look back and forth between your paper and your viewfinder, drawing exactly what you see. Fill the entire paper with your drawing. If you wish, you may color your picture with crayons when you are finished.

Art Materials	THINK SAFETY
Paper or thin cardboard for viewfinders	White drawing paper
Scissors	Pencil
	Crayons

Learning Outcomes

1. How does a viewfinder help an artist to compose a scene?

2. Did you choose a vertical or a horizontal shape for your scene? Why did you choose that shape for your picture?

3. Would the Sloan painting have been better if it were composed in a vertical shape? Why or why not?

10 *The Great American Outdoors*

Observing and Thinking

In the early days of American painting, artists tried hard to copy the **style** and subject matter of European painters. Soon, though, American artists felt the need to paint subjects that were uniquely American. They looked around at the natural beauty of their country and decided that they would record America's landscapes in their art. A **landscape** is a drawing or painting that shows a scene from the natural environment.

The first artists to create a truly American style of landscape painting were the painters of the **Hudson River School**. This small group of artists showed the beauty of New York's Hudson River region in **realistic** paintings. The Hudson River painters did more than just paint what they saw, though. They recorded their own moods and feelings in the scenes they drew and painted from nature.

Later artists carried on the tradition of the Hudson River School. Frederick Church painted scenes of the American landscape that seem almost more than realistic. In his *Twilight in the Wilderness*, he showed the interest many American landscape painters, called **Luminists** (lü'-mə-nəstz), had in the effects of light on clouds and scenery.

Albert Bierstadt painted scenes of the American West. He worked from sketches taken from life, but his paintings were done in his studio. What time of day do you think *Among the Sierra Nevada Mountains, California* shows? How did Bierstadt show the effects of light on the landscape?

Frederick Edwin Church, Twilight in the Wilderness. *1860. Oil on canvas. 40″×64″.*
The Cleveland Museum of Art, Mr. and Mrs. William H. Marlatt Fund.

Albert Bierstadt, Among the Sierra Nevada Mountains, California. *1868. Oil on canvas. 72″ × 120″. National Museum of American Art, Smithsonian Institution. Bequest of Helen Huntington Hull. 1977.107.1*

Creating Art

1. Think about the effects color has on you when you look at a real or painted landscape. How does the Church painting make you feel? How is its feeling different from the feeling of the Bierstadt painting? What time of day do you think each painting shows? Why do you say so?

2. Using black colored construction paper, cut out a **silhouette** of a house or other building and at least one tree on a narrow strip of land. Place the silhouette against different background sheets of such colors as orange, yellow, gray, blue, and purple. What does each combination make you think of? Do any of them make you think of particular feelings, times of day, or weather conditions?

3. Using crayons, colored pencils, or oil pastels, color a piece of white paper with hues that remind you of twilight, the dawn, or a storm. Color your sky so that there is a gradual change of colors from lightest at the bottom of the page to darkest or brightest at the top. When you are satis-

fied with the way your sky looks, paste down your silhouette. Add more silhouette shapes if you like.

Art Materials	THINK SAFETY
Colored construction paper (black and an assortment of colors)	Pencil
	Crayons, oil pastels, or colored pencils
White drawing paper	Scissors
	Paste

Learning Outcomes

1. Who were the first artists to create a truly American style of landscape painting? Who were the Luminists?

2. What kind of sky did you show in your silhouette landscape? What colors did you use to make the sky?

3. In what ways did Church and Bierstadt put mood and feeling into their paintings?

11 **The Best Kind of Park**

Observing and Thinking

Did you know that a park has to be designed, just like a work of art? People who design parks are **landscape architects**. Landscape architects must make very important decisions when they **design**, or plan, a city park. They must decide where roads and paths should go, where trees and bushes should be planted, and how different areas can be separated so that many different kinds of activities can go on at once.

America's first landscape architect was Frederick Law Olmsted. In the 1850s, he and Calvert Vaux designed the famous Central Park in New York. This enormous park includes a lake, playgrounds, gardens, forested areas, and even a zoo. Olmsted believed in making city parks resemble forests or meadows, so that people could feel as though they were "getting away from it all" even in the midst of a large city.

Olmsted's ideas about park planning are still in use today. Parks are designed to be attractive, enjoyable places for people to visit for recreation and relaxation. Yet, they are also designed with practical concerns in mind. Landscape architects have to think about soil erosion, the placement of different recreational areas, and making the best use of space. By making these decisions well, landscape architects can create park areas that truly enrich our lives.

Frederick Law Olmsted.
Courtesy of the New York Historical Society.

Central Park, New York

Central Park, New York

Central Park, New York

Creating Art

1. Think about your local park, a park you have visited or seen pictures of, or a park from your imagination. What would the park of your dreams be like? What kinds of activities could you enjoy at your park? How could your park best serve the needs of your community?

2. Plan out a park design on a piece of drawing paper as though you were making a map of the park. What kinds of plants and trees will your park have? Where will they be planted? Where will you make your roads and footpaths? How will you separate areas for different kinds of activities? Will there be a central part of the park? A lake? A playground? You may need to make a few sketches of your park plan before you are ready to draw your final map.

3. Share your park plan with the rest of the class. Explain the different parts of your park, and why you made the decisions you did in the planning of your park.

Art Materials	
Drawing paper	Colored pencils or crayons (optional)
Pencil	

Learning Outcomes

1. What is the job of a landscape architect in creating a park?

2. How did you decide to separate different areas in your map of your park?

3. What kinds of decisions do landscape architects have to make?

12 Structures That Fit the Environment

Observing and Thinking

Do you think of buildings as examples of art? **Architecture**, the art of designing structures, is one of the oldest art forms. Like other forms of art, it is always changing. Are there any examples of new and unusual architecture in your town or city?

Most of the architecture we see around us is made up of **geometric** shapes and forms. Since the middle of the twentieth century, though, some architects have become dissatisfied with the boxlike structures we live and work in. Frank Lloyd Wright, one of America's greatest architects, felt that structures should fit in with their natural surroundings. He designed many buildings that blended in so well with their natural environments that they seemed like a part of nature themselves. His buildings were based on geometric shapes, but he called them **organic** structures, meaning that they were natural, a part of the land they were built on.

James Hubbell's home in the country is like a living work of art. He, his family, and his friends have been building it for over twenty years. It is made up of many separate structures that blend in with their natural surroundings. There are few perfectly geometric forms in Hubbell's architecture. Instead, his structures are like undersea caves. Hubbell believes that architecture can exist in harmony with nature. Inside and outside, his structures reflect a sense of magic.

Frank Lloyd Wright, Second Herbert Jacobs House, Middleton, Wisconsin. 1948. Photograph copyright Ezra Stoller © ESTO.

James Hubbell, Home in Julian, California. West side: boys' bungalow. *Photograph copyright © 1985 by Otto B. Rigan.*

Oscar Niemeyer, House for architect, Rio de Janeiro, Brazil. *1953–1954. Photograph courtesy The Museum of Modern Art, New York.*

Creating Art

1. Think about a place where you would like to live. It could be in a tree, in the middle of a jungle, under the ocean, in the desert, or even on another planet. Imagine what the place would have to look like to blend in with its surroundings. What kind of shelter would it have to provide to protect you from your environment?

2. Draw a design for a structure that would fit the environment you chose. Try to make your building look unlike any other building you have ever seen. It should blend in perfectly with the natural setting you chose. Try to avoid making it too geometric in shape. Remember to draw the setting as well as the structure.

3. When your design is finished, color your drawing with crayons or colored pencils.

Share your architectural design with the rest of the class.

Art Materials

White drawing paper	Crayons or
Pencil	colored pencils

Learning Outcomes

1. What is organic architecture? How is it different from most of the architecture we see around us?

2. How did the structure you designed fit in with the natural setting you chose?

3. Which of the structures shown in this lesson fits in best with its environment? Which would you most like to live in?

13 *We Decorate the Things We Use*

Observing and Thinking

Whenever lines, shapes, or colors repeat, a **pattern** is made. You see patterns everywhere, every day of your life, even if you don't realize it. There is pattern in the stripes on a tabby cat, the bricks in a brick wall, the shadows cast by a picket fence, the lines made in newly plowed soil, and even in the arrangement of products on the shelves of your grocery store. Some patterns are planned and regular, like the pattern of tiles in a bathroom. Other patterns, such as footprints in the sand, don't have a regular repeating design.

People of all times and cultures have used patterns to decorate the things around them. Patterns add beauty, interest, and variety to our lives. Even useful, everyday objects can seem like works of art if they are decorated with patterns. Fabrics, wallpaper, tablecloths, ceramics, even vehicles: you can find patterns on all of these things, and more.

In this lesson, you will make a printing stamp out of clay and use it to create your own pattern on a piece of paper.

Sevres porcelain Caberet Service. 1813. Enamel/gilt decorations. Gift of Mrs. Katrina H. Becker, in memory of her parents, Mr. and Mrs. Charles V. Hickox. Cooper-Hewitt Museum, New York.

John Lennon Psychedelic Rolls-Royce. *Permission granted by Ripley International, Inc., 1986.*

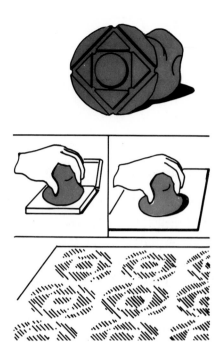

Creating Art

1. Take a small lump of clay and form it into a printing stamp with a handle. The printing surface of your stamp can be any shape, but it should be perfectly flat.

2. Make a design in the printing surface of your stamp. You can press an object into the clay, such as a seashell, fork, or bolt, or you can make deep grooves with a pencil or other object. Impress or carve your design deeply into the clay.

3. Press your clay stamp onto a paint-soaked pad, or paint it with a brush. Practice printing on a piece of newsprint. Press gently with the stamp, hold it for a few seconds, then lift it up. You should have made a clear print of your design.

4. On a piece of white or colored paper, make a repeating pattern with your stamp. You can make your design in a straight repeating line or vary the placement of your design to create an irregular pattern.

5. When your pattern is completed, let it dry. For what purpose will your patterned paper be used? Wrapping a gift? Decorating a can to make a pencil holder? Perhaps you will make a cover for this book. Only you can decide.

Art Materials

Oil-based clay	Water, paper towels
Newsprint	
White or colored paper for printing	Water container
	Newspaper
Tempera paint	Objects to press into clay
Brush or paint pad	

Learning Outcomes

1. What is a pattern? Give some examples of patterns in your home or classroom.

2. How did you create a pleasing pattern with your clay printing stamp? What other objects could you use for printing?

3. What kinds of useful objects that you own could be improved with patterns?

27

14 Be a Creative Weaver

Observing and Thinking

You can see the beauty of woven products not only in man-made things but also in the creations of nature. Study the dewy spider web—a delicate form of **weaving**. Notice how the spider has attached its web. Now look at the weaver working at her **loom**. How is the loom like the spider's web?

All weaving is done on looms. Looms can be made of many things. Straws, cardboard, wood, branches, and huge man-made machine looms like the ones used in factories are all types of looms. Your fingers can even serve as a loom!

A loom is a framework made to hold the warp of a weaving in place. The warp is the first set of threads or **fibers** attached lengthwise, or vertically, to the loom. The other set of fibers is called the **weft**. The weft is woven at right angles to the warp, creating the pattern or **design** of a weaving. Many objects you can find in nature may be used as part of the weft. Feathers, burrs, leaves, weeds, dried plants, and shells can be woven into your warp to add texture and **variety**.

In this lesson, you will use fibers and various natural objects to create your own original weaving on a very natural loom: the branch of a tree.

28

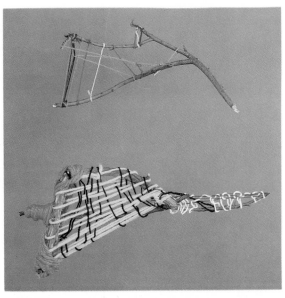

Creating Art

1. Find a fallen branch from a tree or a piece of driftwood that has a "Y" shape or forked part. Branches with rough bark will work best. Collect natural objects and left-over yarn or other fibers from home to weave on your branch.

2. Wind string or yarn around the widest part of your branch and knot it securely. Then lace the yarn across and around the opposite branch. Continue looping your yarn until you have filled your loom with warp fibers that are about the same distance apart from each other. Tie the yarn around the branch in a secure knot when you have finished making your warp.

3. Weave the weft with your fibers and natural objects. Think about creating a design by repeating colors and textures in your weaving to form an interesting pattern. You can change your pattern—you do not always have to weave one fiber under and over another. Experiment with various patterns, and see what looks best.

4. Remember, this isn't a flat weaving. You can hang objects from your warp, cross a

warp to a different branch, or do anything you want to create an interesting **three-dimensional** effect. Display your weaving when it is done. Remember that your branch loom is a part of your weaving. Unlike other looms, you won't be taking the weaving off this loom.

Art Materials

A branch from a tree or a piece of driftwood	Scissors
Colored yarn, string, and other fibers	Natural objects for the weft: yarn, feathers, weeds, dried plants, etc.

Learning Outcomes

1. Define the terms *weaving, loom, fibers, warp,* and *weft.*

2. What elements of design did you use to create the effect you wanted?

3. Point out the part of your weaving that has the most interest or appeal.

15 *American Nature Artists*

Observing and Thinking

When the New World was first discovered, the people of Europe were curious to learn what the new land looked like. Because photography had not yet been invented, artists had to "take pictures" of the plants and animals that existed in the Americas by drawing and painting them accurately. Long after that time, artists continued to find the native plants and animals of America fascinating subjects for art. These **artist-naturalists** were as much scientists as artists. They devoted their lives to making pictures of the wildlife of their native land.

The most famous of these artist-naturalists was John James Audubon. One hundred and fifty years ago, Audubon traveled throughout the United States to observe and paint the birds of America. He also took detailed notes of their habits. In this way, he made valuable contributions to science.

Abbott and Gerald Thayer were other important nature artists. Abbott Thayer discovered that animals have colors and **patterns** that help them blend into their surroundings. His son Gerald's painting of a ruffed grouse shows the truth of this observation. Martin Johnson Heade was a painter of American landscapes. He became interested in the hummingbirds of South America and traveled there to paint and study them.

John James Audubon, Gyrfalcon. 1833. Watercolor. 38½" × 25⅝". Courtesy of The New-York Historical Society, New York.

Gerald M. Thayer, Male Ruffed Grouse in the Forest. Watercolor on paper. 19¾" × 20". The Metropolitan Museum of Art, Rogers Fund, 1916. (16.167)

Martin Johnson Heade, Orchids, Passion Flowers, and Hummingbird. *1865. Oil. 19½″ × 13½″. Collection of Whitney Museum of American Art. Gift of Mr. Robert C. Graham in honor of John I. H. Baur.*

Creating Art

1. Study a photograph of a bird. If you can, find several photographs of the bird taken from different positions. Look up some information about the bird you chose in an encyclopedia. Jot down some notes about the bird's habits.

2. On a large piece of colored construction paper (light blue, gray, tan, or green would be best), lightly sketch a picture of your bird. Make your picture fairly large. When you are satisfied with your sketch, color your bird with oil pastels. Let parts of your paper show through so that they become part of the drawing. Add details with colored pencils. You can also create some interesting effects by scratching away parts of the pastel with a sharp object, such as a paper clip. Try to show textures on your bird. Draw the bird's environment, too, by adding such details as grass, water, or flowers.

Art Materials

Colored construction paper (light colors)	Oil pastels
	Colored pencils
Pencil	Paper clips

Learning Outcomes

1. How are artist-naturalists like scientists?

2. What details did you include in your bird drawing? How did you show the texture of the bird's body?

3. Which of the paintings shown here seems most scientific? Which seems most like a painting you would find in a museum?

Exploring Art

Have Sketchbook, Will Travel

Have you ever admired a work of art and wished that art was as easy for you as it was for the artist? Yet art is hard work. Even the greatest artists had to practice for years to become the best they could be. To an artist, art is not something to be done every once in a while. Art is a skill to be practiced frequently.

One way that an artist practices and learns more about art is by keeping a **sketchbook**. In their sketchbooks, artists record what they see in the world around them. To them, sketching is a necessary exercise similar to practicing the scales on a piano or warming up to play baseball.

You can make your own sketchbook by folding and stapling drawing paper together. If you want to make a **bound** sketchbook, ask your teacher for instructions. Your sketchbook will remind you to draw often.

Draw what you see and what you know. Use pencils, colored markers, crayons, or whatever **medium** you wish. Don't worry about what your drawings look like. You don't even have to show them to anyone else. As long as you use drawing as a way to learn to observe the world around you more closely, you will be learning what is perhaps the artist's greatest skill: how to see.

Umberto Boccioni, Study for The City Rises. 1910. Crayon and chalk, sheet: 23⅛″ × 34⅛″. Collection, The Museum of Modern Art, New York. Mrs. Simon Guggenheim Fund.

Review

Using What You Have Learned

Charles Sheeler was an American painter and photographer. He was interested in **architecture** and was well-known for his paintings of buildings. He painted *City Interior* during one of his most **realistic** periods. Study *City Interior* as an art critic might.

Charles Sheeler, City Interior. 1936. *Aqueous adhesive and oil on composition board. 22⅛" × 27". Worcester Art Museum. Museum purchase.*

1. Is this painting made up of mostly **free-form** or **geometric** shapes? Point out examples of the kinds of shapes Sheeler used in this painting.

2. In what shape is this painting **composed**, or designed? Would it have been better if Sheeler had composed it in a different shape? Why or why not?

3. What is the **center of interest** in Sheeler's painting? What leads your eyes to it?

4. What kinds of **lines** do you see in this painting? Where are lines and **shapes** repeated to form **patterns**?

5. How did the artist show different **textures** in his work?

6. What evidence do you see that Sheeler was a careful observer of his environment? How is this painting like a photograph? How is it different?

Unit 2

Communicating Moods and Messages

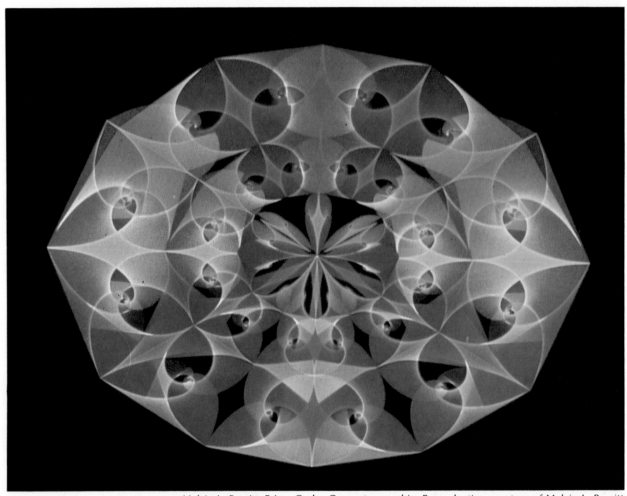

Melvin L. Prueitt, Prime Cycle. Computer graphic. Reproduction courtesy of Melvin L. Prueitt, IS-2, Los Alamos National Laboratory, author of Art and the Computer, McGraw-Hill, 1984.

We live in a world filled with **images**. The shapes, forms, and colors of the modern world are everywhere we turn. Often, the images we see are **symbols** that stand for ideas, objects, feelings, and experiences. With symbols, we communicate the things that are important to us, and that we want to share with others. The visual images around us express the society in which we live, and in turn influence the way we think and feel.

Anonymous, Wurlitzer Jukebox. 1945. National Museum of American History, Smithsonian Institution, Washington, D.C.

Art is a universal form of communication. Throughout human history, people have expressed themselves through art. Even when the main purpose of most art forms was practical, people recognized the **expressive** power of art. They created artworks that not only served special functions, but also told of human needs and experiences. They were concerned not just with an object's purpose, but with its beauty as well, and with its ability to communicate human feelings and interests that others could share.

Every work of art helps us to learn a little more about what it means to be a human being. The art of today fulfills the same human needs as the art of thousands of years ago, even though it takes different forms. If you look at artworks from past ages, you will find that the messages they speak have not been lost. The art of the past can speak to us as clearly as the art of the present.

Perhaps no other people in history have been as surrounded by visual images as we are today. From billboards and store window displays to books and magazines, from television and movies to bright city lights and computer art, we boldly proclaim our fast-paced, technological society. Look at the colorful images all around you. Do they express what it means to be a person living in the world in this time? Do they influence the way you think and feel?

Frank Stella, Kastūra. 1979. Oil and epoxy on aluminum, wire mesh. 9'7" × 7'8" × 30". Collection, The Museum of Modern Art, New York. Acquired through Mr. and Mrs. Victor Ganz, Mr. and Mrs. Donald H. Peters, and Mr. and Mrs. Charles Zadok Funds.

16 One-Color Collage

Observing and Thinking

Have you ever looked at the world through red-tinted glasses? Everything seemed to show up as **variations** of red. You may not have known it, but you were seeing a **monochrome** world.

When you see the word part *mono*, you know that it means *one* or *single*. *Monochrome* means a single color. Some artists make monochrome paintings or drawings, using a single color and its variations.

Colors, or **hues**, can be changed in many ways. Adding black, white, or gray is a common way to change a color. You can add black to a hue and make a **shade**. You can add white and make a **tint**. When you add gray to a color, you make a **tone**. Artists may use just one color and its variations to unify different parts of a drawing, painting, or sculpture into a pleasing whole.

Look at Picasso's *The Blind Man's Meal*. What feeling do you get from this painting? It was created during what is called Picasso's Blue Period. The paintings he made at this time focused on feelings of loneliness and sorrow. Why do you think he chose blue to express these feelings? Can you see how, by repeating and varying the same color, Picasso created **unity** in his painting?

*Pablo Picasso, The Blind Man's Meal.
1903. Oil on canvas. 37½" × 37¼".
The Metropolitan Museum of Art.
Gift of Mr. and Mrs. Ira Haupt, 1950.*

Creating Art

1. Select one color, or hue, that you want to use in a **collage**. A collage is a **two-dimensional** design made of materials such as paper and fabrics glued to a flat background. Cut out many sizes and shapes of the color you have selected from magazines. Do not cut out objects, but instead **geometric** and **free-form** shapes. Cut out more pieces than you will need so that you can choose the shapes and sizes that will make the most interesting design.

2. Arrange several of the clippings you have selected on a sheet of white paper. Arrange and rearrange the pieces two or three times. Organize the pieces so that they create an interesting design.

3. When you have made an arrangement that you like, paste all the pieces of your monochrome design on the piece of paper. When you are through, you can use a picture of a person, an object, or the letters that spell out the color's name as

the **center of interest**. Do not put the object or word directly in the center of your picture. Instead, place it so that it is off to one side in **asymmetrical balance**.

Art Materials	THINK SAFETY
White paper	Pictures from magazines
Paste	
Scissors	Paper towels

Learning Outcomes

1. What does *monochrome* mean? Name three ways you can vary a color.

2. How did you select a color and arrange your clippings to make a good design? What do you like best about your one-color collage?

3. Why do you think that artists make monochrome paintings? What different effects can artists achieve with monochromes?

17 *Geometric Quilts*

Observing and Thinking

What do you use to cover your bed in cold weather? Today, it's very simple for us to go out and buy a bedspread in a store when we need one. But years ago, people had to make all the things they used. Instead of blankets, they made and used **quilts** that were hand-sewn. Because cloth was very hard to get, people used every little scrap. Often, they cut scraps of cloth into **geometric shapes** and fitted them together to make an interesting **design**. They repeated the design over and over again to make a quilt that had an interesting pattern. Sometimes they gave these designs special names and let other people use them in their quilts. These designs were passed from generation to generation.

One type of quilt that people used to make was called a "nine-patch quilt." It was made of squares that were each divided into nine sections. Can you find the nine patches in the quilt square shown on the next page?

Look at the painting called *The Quilting Party*. Can you find the big quilt that people are making? When there was a big job to be done, like harvesting a crop, building a house, or making a quilt, early Americans often worked together.

In this lesson, you will make a geometric nine-patch quilt square, using just two colors to achieve **unity**.

Artist unidentified, The Quilting Party. ca. 1854–1875. Oil and pencil on paper adhered to plywood. 19¼″ × 26⅛″. Abby Aldrich Rockefeller Folk Art Center, Williamsburg, Virginia.

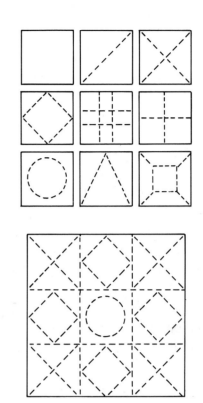

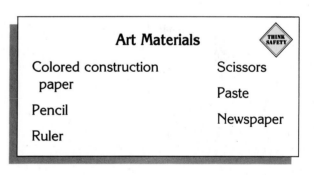

Creating Art

1. Use your ruler to divide a colored paper square into nine equal parts, three across and three up and down.

2. You can make many geometric shapes out of your nine parts. As in the example shown above, you can choose one or more ways to cut out and combine squares, triangles, diamond shapes, and other geometric shapes for your nine-patch quilt square.

3. Arrange your geometric shapes on a "nine-patch" square that is a different color. Paste the pieces in place. Do you see how using just two colors helps to **unify** your design? Try putting your quilt square with other quilt squares made by classmates. How do they look together?

Art Materials	THINK SAFETY
Colored construction paper	Scissors
Pencil	Paste
Ruler	Newspaper

Learning Outcomes

1. What is a quilt? Why did people make quilts? How were quilts designed?

2. How did you arrange the geometric pieces in your design?

3. What other decorative crafts can you name? Are any of them created by groups of people working together?

18 Imagineering with Color

Observing and Thinking

Do you like to perform experiments? Artists, like scientists, often experiment to discover new **techniques**, or methods, of using their tools and materials. Painters often use paints in ways they haven't tried before, mixing new colors and putting colors together in interesting ways. They also experiment with different ways of using one of their most important tools: the paintbrush.

You can use your paintbrush and paints in many different ways to create paintings that have a variety of **lines**, **textures**, and **shapes**. You can see many different kinds of **brushstrokes** in the painting by Vasily Kandinsky. Kandinsky, an early **abstract** painter, believed that painting is a personal expression that comes from deep inside the artist. He would often let his paintings simply "happen." He painted quickly, using bright colors and swirling brushstrokes with lots of movement. Can you tell how some of the brushstrokes in his painting were made? Compare his style to that of Samuel Francis, whose painting *Towards Disappearance, II* is shown below.

The way a painter uses brushes and paints is one part of his or her **style**. You can start to develop your own style by practicing different techniques of using your brush and paints. Some of the ways you can do this are shown on the next page.

Vasily Kandinsky, Painting Number 201. 1914 Summer. Oil on canvas. 64¼" × 48¼". Collection, The Museum of Modern Art, New York. Nelson A. Rockefeller Fund.

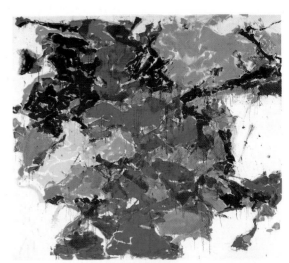

Sam Francis, Towards Disappearance, II. 1958. Oil on canvas. 9'½" × 10'5⅞". Collection, The Museum of Modern Art, New York. Blanchette Rockefeller Fund.

Wet brush on dry paper

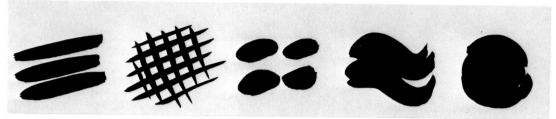

Dry brush on dry paper

Wet brush on wet paper

Creating Art

1. Try some different techniques for using your paints and brush. Make some experiments on paper. Paint quickly. Don't be afraid to use the motion of your entire arm as you paint. Clean your brush thoroughly after each color that you use. Do you prefer any techniques over others?

2. Now you are ready to paint an "unplanned" painting that expresses deep thoughts or feelings. Don't think about what you are going to paint. Simply experiment with your brush and with different colors. Use the techniques you liked best from your experiments. Use bright, pure colors. Try using a nearly dry brush. What effects do you get? If you want, add black lines to your painting to bring out different shapes that the brushstrokes have made. What does your painting express?

Art Materials	
White drawing paper	Water, paper towels
Tempera paints	Water container
Brushes	Newspaper
Mixing tray	

Learning Outcomes

1. Why do artists experiment with different techniques of painting?

2. What kinds of brushstrokes did you use in your painting? What techniques did you like best?

3. What do you think the paintings by Kandinsky and Francis are trying to express? Give reasons for your answer.

19 Seeing Color Relationships

Observing and Thinking

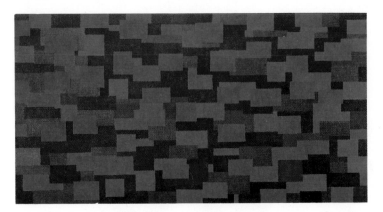

Ad Reinhardt, Number 88, 1950 (Blue). *1950. Oil on canvas. 75" × 144". Hirshhorn Museum and Sculpture Garden, Smithsonian Institution.*

Did you know that colors are related to one another in different ways? When colors have something in common, they appear close to one another on the color wheel. For example, orange is made of red and yellow, so it appears near them. When colors are like one another in some way, we say that they are related or **analogous** (ə-nal'-ə-gəs) **colors**. Artists often use analogous colors to express moods and feelings in their artwork. Using these related colors together can create a strong, or **dominant**, effect in a painting. What is the dominant effect of Ad Reinhardt's *Number 88, 1950 (Blue),* shown above?

Complementary colors are pairs of color opposites. These colors appear directly across from each other on the color wheel. They are sometimes called **contrasting** colors, because of the great difference between them. Artists will place complementary color pairs side by side to create exciting, dramatic effects. This is because complementary colors make each other seem brighter and bolder when they are placed next to each other.

Study the painting by Stanton Macdonald-Wright on this page. Do you see where he used analogous colors together? Did he place any complementary colors together to achieve interesting contrasts?

In this lesson, you will paint a natural or man-made object, using either all analogous or all complementary colors.

Stanton Macdonald-Wright, Conception Synchromy. *1914. Oil on canvas. 36" × 30⅛". Hirshhorn Museum and Sculpture Garden, Smithsonian Institution.*

42

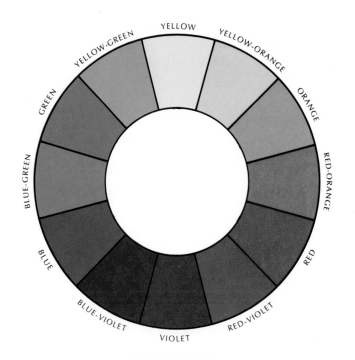

COLOR WHEEL

Creating Art

1. Sketch an object from life. It can be a man-made or natural object. A musical instrument, such as a horn, would make a good subject. So would a football helmet, a small sculpture, or a plastic model. Your drawing should fill the paper.

2. Choose three analogous or two complementary colors to paint your picture. You may add varying amounts of white to your colors as well. If you want to create harmony in your painting, try using analogous colors. What kinds of colors would you use to create a feeling of excitement?

3. Paint your picture. Fill in all the spaces with color. When the paint has dried, you may use a black marker to fill all the lines between the shapes to achieve **unity**.

4. Display your picture with other pictures of the object that use different colors. How are the effects different in each painting?

Art Materials	
White drawing paper	Water, paper towels
Pencil	Water container
Tempera paints	Object to draw
Brush	Black marker
Mixing tray	Newspapers

Learning Outcomes

1. What are some of the effects an artist can achieve with analogous and complementary colors?

2. Why did you select the colors you used in your painting? Did you achieve the effect you expected?

3. Describe the feelings or mood you experienced when looking at the paintings by Macdonald-Wright and Reinhardt.

20 A Color Is a Mood

Observing and Thinking

Have you ever heard of warm and cool colors? Red, yellow, orange, and their related colors are called **warm colors** because they remind people of energy, light, and heat. They also make people think of warm feelings, like happiness and joy. Blue, green, violet, and their related colors are called **cool colors**. Why do you think so? What moods or feelings do they remind you of?

Artists often use hues called **neutral colors**. These are colors you won't find in the rainbow. Black, white, gray, and brown are neutral colors. They can be mixed with warm and cool colors to make warm and cool neutrals. The warm colors can be mixed with neutrals to form warm neutrals. The cool colors can be mixed with neutrals to form cool neutrals. When black is mixed with colors, it makes warm or cool **shades**. When white is mixed with colors, it makes warm or cool **tints**. How do you think neutrals, tints, and shades can add to the overall mood of a painting or other work of art?

Look at the paintings by William Sydney Mount and Pablo Picasso. Which painting is made with warm colors? What is the mood of this painting? Which painting is made with cool colors? How does it make you feel? Do you see neutral colors in either painting? Are they warm or cool neutrals?

William Sydney Mount, The Banjo Player. *c. 1858. 25" × 30".*
The Detroit Institute of Arts. Gift of Dexter M. Ferry, Jr.

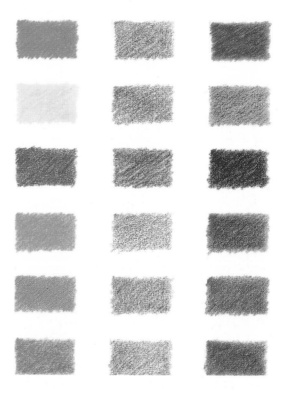

Pablo Picasso, The Old Guitarist. *1903. Oil on panel. 47 ¾" × 32½". Helen Birch Bartlett Memorial Collection. No. 26.253*

Creating Art

1. Think of a mood or feeling you would like to show in a scene. Would your mood be best expressed in warm or cool colors? What kinds of scenes would look best in all warm or all cool colors? You can use people, animals, or objects in your scene, if you wish.

2. When you have decided on a mood and a scene, draw it on light-colored paper that is either a warm or cool color. Then choose three warm or three cool colors and the neutral colors white, black, gray, and brown. These are the only colors you may use to make your artwork. Color your picture with all warm or all cool colors. Use the neutral colors in your picture as well. Experiment by blending the neutral colors with your other colors to see what effects you can achieve. You can make the warm or cool background color of your paper add to the overall effect of your picture by letting parts of it show through.

Art Materials

Colored paper (Light warm and cool colors)	Oil pastels or crayons
Pencil	Paper towels

Learning Outcomes

1. What are warm, cool, and neutral colors? How do they express various moods?

2. Did you use warm or cool colors in your picture? How did you use neutral colors?

3. How are the paintings by Mount and Picasso similar? How are they different?

45

21 *Still Life with Flowers*

Observing and Thinking

Have you ever picked a variety of flowers and arranged them carefully in a vase? Artists often paint pictures of objects put together in pleasing **compositions**. A drawing or painting that features objects rather than people or scenes is called a **still life**.

Flowers are one of the most popular subjects of still life paintings. Because flowers come in an endless variety of colors, shapes, and textures, they are interesting for artists to observe and paint.

The French artist Odilon Redon (rə-dō′) created many still life paintings of flowers. He had studied botany, the science of plant life, and knew a lot about flowers. In his still life paintings, Redon showed that he understood color and its uses. He realized that there were many **variations** of a color in a single flower. He would change a bright red to a light red or pink **tint** by adding a bit of white. If he wanted to create a darker hue, called a **shade**, he would add black to red. Can you also see the use of tints and shades in the painting by Edouard Manet (ma-nā′)?

In this lesson, you will use tints and shades to create a still life painting of flowers.

Odilon Redon, Flowers in a Vase. *c. 1910. Canvas. 22″ × 15½″. National Gallery of Art, Washington, D.C. Ailsa Mellon Bruce Collection.*

Edouard Manet, Flowers in a Crystal Vase. *c. 1882. Canvas. 12⅞″ × 9⅝″ National Gallery of Art, Washington, D.C. Ailsa Mellon Bruce Collection.*

46

Creating Art

1. Study a vase of flowers. Notice all the colors. Are the leaves and stems all the same color green? Is the vase all one color?

2. Plan your painting. Will your paper be **horizontal** or **vertical**? Your vase can be in the center of the paper or off to one side in **asymmetrical** balance. Lightly sketch in the shapes of the vase and flowers and the lines of the stems.

3. Mix shades and tints of green tempera paint for the stems and leaves. Then mix all the shades and tints of colors you will be using on your flowers and for the vase. Your paint should be thick.

4. Paint the vase, then the stems and leaves. Use many kinds of brushstrokes. You can paint darker colors first, then let them dry and paint lighter colors over them.

5. Use many tints and shades with your pure colors. Roll the brush around on the paper to make a flower that looks like a rose. "Stamp in" petals in a circle with your brush. Make flowers in many different ways, and in many different colors.

Art Materials	
White paper	Mixing tray
Pencil	Water container
Vase of flowers	Newspapers
Tempera paints	Water, paper towels
Brushes	

Learning Outcomes

1. What are tints and shades of colors? How are they made?

2. How did you use your colors and your brush to make your flowers look real?

3. What do you like about the Redon and Manet paintings? How did these artists use tints and shades in their paintings?

22 Black Lines

Observing and Thinking

Sometimes, artists use bold, black lines to surround parts of their artwork. In stained-glass windows, hundreds of pieces of brightly colored glass are put together like a jigsaw puzzle. The lines you see are the strips of lead that hold all the pieces of glass together. They are also part of the **design**. They **unify** the shapes and colors of the window.

An artist named Georges Rouault (rü-ō′) worked in a shop that fixed stained-glass windows when he was a young man. His paintings often look like the stained-glass windows he worked on. In *The Old King*, below, Rouault used heavy black lines to surround shapes of jewel-like colors. How do the lines and colors unify the artwork?

Georges Rouault, The Old King. *1916–1938. Oil on canvas. 30¼″ × 21¼″. Museum of Art, Carnegie Institute. Patrons Art Fund, 40.1*

Other artists have used heavy lines to surround objects in their paintings. The black lines separate the parts of the paintings from their backgrounds. In what other ways can artists create unity?

In this lesson, you will make a picture that achieves unity with black lines.

Creating Art

1. With chalk, sketch an animal or person on a piece of black construction paper. Keep the drawing simple. Make it like a stained-glass window, divided up into shapes.

2. Go over the lines of your drawing with white glue. Use glue from a bottle to make a drawing of white lines on the black paper. Let the glue dry.

3. With chalk or oil pastels, completely fill in the shapes of your drawing. Use pressure on the chalk or pastel so that your colors will be intense. Use your fingers to spread the colors so that they come up to the lines of hardened glue.

4. When you have finished, you should see black where the **transparent** glue lines surround the shapes in your drawing.

5. Display the many black-line drawings on a wall in a brightly colored arrangement.

Anonymous, Queen Kunigunde (detail from stained-glass windows in Church of St. Leonhard, Lavanthal). 1340–50. Pot metal glass. 38½" × 17½". The Metropolitan Museum of Art, The Cloisters Collection, 1965.

Art Materials		THINK SAFETY
Black paper	White glue	
White chalk	Newspapers	
Colored chalk or oil pastels	Paper towels	

Learning Outcomes

1. How do black lines help artists create unity in their artwork?

2. How would you describe the effect of the black lines in your design?

3. How is Rouault's *The Old King* like a stained-glass window? What do you like or dislike about this effect?

49

23 Transparent and Opaque

Observing and Thinking

The pictures shown in this lesson were painted by American artists in the late 1800s. What do you see in the two paintings that is similar? What do you see that is different?

Winslow Homer painted pictures that showed the American life of his time. In *The Blue Boat,* he used **watercolors** to show the shimmering light on the water and the soft shapes of the clouds and landscape. Watercolors are **transparent**, which means that you can see through them. They are a watery, thin paint that can create soft, fuzzy effects. Homer overlapped some of his colors to make new ones. He let white paper show

through in some places to show highlights. Can you find where he did these two things?

Thomas Eakins also painted scenes of American life. He was a **realistic** painter who is considered one of America's greatest artists. He used **oil paints** to make his pictures. Oil paints are **opaque**. This means that you cannot see through them. Unlike watercolors, oil paints hide the colors underneath them. Artists who use watercolors can overlap colors to create new colors as they paint. Oil painters must mix all their colors first.

In this lesson, you will make a watercolor painting of the subject of your choice.

Winslow Homer, The Blue Boat. Watercolor on paper. 14¾″ × 21¼″. Bequest of William Sturgis Bigelow. Courtesy, Museum of Fine Arts, Boston.

Thomas Eakins, Biglin Brothers Turning the Stake. *1873. Oil on canvas. 40¼″ × 60¼″. The Cleveland Museum of Art, Hinman B. Hurlbut Collection.*

Creating Art

1. Think about a subject that you would like to paint in watercolors. You can draw a scene, a still life, or even a person. Earlier sketches you have made may give you some ideas. Choose a subject that is best suited to these watery, transparent colors. Draw it lightly in pencil.

2. Use a big brush to spread water all over your paper. You will first paint the background of your picture. Load a small brush with lots of color from your watercolor box. Spread the color on the wet paper. You will see the color spread and get fuzzy around the edges. Let the color spread and then dry for a few minutes.

3. Rinse your brush often, especially when you want to change colors. Paint in the largest and lightest-colored areas of your picture first. Save the details for last. Do not worry if some of your colors spread. The beauty of watercolor is in its soft, watery effects. As some of the areas dry, overlap colors. Paint dark over light. Why can't you paint light over dark?

4. Let your paper dry. Now you can use your watercolors to add some lines. Do not outline everything. You may only want to add a few lines to sharpen the **image** in your painting. Stop every now and then and step back to look at your painting from a distance. When you are satisfied, give your painting a title.

Art Materials

White paper	Water container
Brushes	Water, paper towels
Watercolor paints	
Pencil	Newspapers

Learning Outcomes

1. How are transparent colors different from colors that are opaque?

2. Which colors did you overlap in your painting?

3. What do the paintings by Homer and Eakins tell you about life in that time?

51

24 A Memory Box

Observing and Thinking

Do you have something that you don't use anymore, but that you don't want to throw away? Many people keep things that remind them of the past. Sometimes they keep old toys, dolls, or sports equipment that they once used. They may keep letters, ticket stubs, or postcards. Things that we keep to help us remember events of the past are called **memorabilia** (mem-ə-rə-bil'-ē-a).

Two American artists who painted collections of memorabilia were William Harnett and John Peto. These two men were friends who spent their lives making **realistic** paintings that were as true-to-life as photographs.

William M. Harnett, My Gems. 1888. Wood. 18″ × 14″. National Gallery of Art, Washington, D.C. Gift of the Avalon Foundation.

They used everyday objects and arranged them into interesting **compositions**. Both artists taught themselves to draw and paint. Sometimes people thought that works by Peto were really by Harnett. Yet their styles were different. Harnett in particular used tiny brushstrokes and made sharp, crisp edges on objects he painted. What are some of the qualities of Peto's work, *Letter Rack*? Discuss similarities and differences between this work and *My Gems*.

Using a kind of **three-dimensional** art form called **assemblage** (ə-sem'-blij), you will create your own memorabilia collection.

John Frederick Peto, Letter Rack. *Oil on canvas. 23½″ × 19½″. The Metropolitan Museum of Art, George A. Hearn Fund, 1955. 55.176*

Creating Art

1. An assemblage is an artist's collection of odds and ends arranged to create a three-dimensional work of art. You will make an assemblage of objects to form a "memory box" that tells something about you.

2. Start with a cardboard box that is a few inches deep and square or rectangular in shape. If you can't find a box of this shape, a shoebox will do. Paint the inside and outside of the box in a dark tempera paint color, like black or brown. The dark background color will help **unify** the objects of your assemblage.

3. Bring to class a collection of objects that expresses parts of your past or present life. Some examples are used stamps or baseball cards, bottle caps, natural objects like seashells or dried weeds, ticket stubs, bicycle reflectors, buttons, scraps of fabric, and tiny, cheap toys. Select objects that have contrasting shapes, textures, and colors.

4. Experiment with different arrangements of these objects. Try to create a pleasing composition on the inside of your box. When you have made an arrangement that you like, glue the parts down. Let everything dry, and display your three-dimensional still life assemblage.

Art Materials	
Cardboard box	Mixing tray
Collection of odds and ends	White glue
Tempera paint	Water container
Brush	Paper towels
	Newspapers

Learning Outcomes

1. What is memorabilia? Name two American artists who painted memorabilia.

2. Explain how the objects you selected for your memory box reflect your present life and personal history.

3. Which objects in the paintings by Harnett and Peto are things that might remind people of the past?

53

25 Number and Letter Shapes

Observing and Thinking

Place your hand on a piece of blank paper. What do you see? The solid **form** of your hand makes a hand shape on your paper. Surrounding your hand, and between your fingers, there is empty space. This **negative space** has its own shape, and it helps to show up and balance the **positive space** of your hand's shape. If you look around you, you will see shapes and spaces everywhere. Every filled positive space is balanced by the empty, or negative, space that surrounds it.

Artists know that negative spaces are just as important as positive spaces. When artists arrange, or **compose**, their pictures, they use negative background space to balance and **unify** the shapes they put on paper.

The various shapes of numbers and letters show how positive and negative spaces work together. Study the ways artists have used positive and negative spaces with numbers and letters in this lesson. Does all the artwork shown here look carefully planned to you? How do the artists use negative background space to make their arrangements of number and letter shapes stand out?

In this lesson, you will make a composition using number, letter, and **abstract** shapes cut from colored paper.

Stuart Davis, *Visa. 1951. Oil on canvas. 40" × 52". Collection, The Museum of Modern Art, New York. Gift of Mrs. Gertrude A. Mellon.*

Robert Indiana, The X-5. *1963. Oil on canvas.*
108" × 108". Five panels, each 36" × 36". Collection
of Whitney Museum of American Art. Purchase.

Paula Scher, The Best of Jazz/CBS
Records, *poster. Reproduced with the*
permission of Paula Scher, Koppel &
Scher, New York.

Creating Art

1. Select several colors of construction paper. You may want to use bright **contrasting colors**, as Stuart Davis did in *Visa*. Use one sheet of paper in the color of your choice for your background.

2. On the other sheets of colored paper, sketch the shapes of numbers and letters, as well as some abstract shapes. You may want to spell out your name or a word. Carefully cut out your shapes. Your teacher will show you how to cut out the centers of letters without ruining the paper. Make all of your shapes in different sizes and colors to add interest to your artwork.

3. Arrange your shapes against the background. Move them around until you have an arrangement that you like. You may want to **overlap** some of the shapes. What are some of the things you can do to give your composition balance and unity?

4. When you are satisfied with your arrangement, glue the pieces in place. Let the glue dry, and display your art. Give your composition a title.

Art Materials ◆ THINK SAFETY

Colored
construction paper

Scissors

Pencil

White glue

Learning Outcomes

1. How do artists use negative space in composing works of art?

2. How did you create balance and unity in your artwork?

3. Point out the negative spaces in your artwork. Why must artists understand positive and negative space?

26 Poster Talk

Observing and Thinking

Have you ever seen a poster that caused you to stop and look at it more closely? Posters, as well as covers of record albums, magazines, and books, are created by **graphic designers**. If you have ever been persuaded by the message on a poster, the graphic designer did his or her work well.

Many of the posters we see around us are examples of **advertising art**. Graphic artists who create advertisements make a science of their work. They study the effects of advertising on people to find out the most effective ways to communicate their advertising messages to the public.

In our fast-moving world, graphic designers have only seconds to get their messages across. Like all artists, they must plan a **center of interest** for their artwork, so that they can draw people's attention to the message of the poster. To what part of the *E.T.* poster are your eyes immediately drawn? How did the artist make this the center of interest?

Graphic designers try to attract our attention in many ways. Sometimes they use startling **images**, such as this rainbow-colored zebra. Other posters catch our attention because the message is simple and direct, as in the *Endangered* poster.

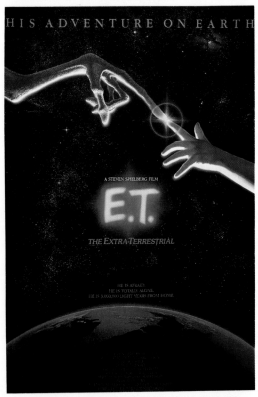

Copyright © by Universal Pictures, a Division of Universal City Studios, Inc. Courtesy of MCA Publishing Rights, a Division of MCA, Inc.

Marvin Mattelson, To Be Good Enough. Poster for the School of Visual Arts. Courtesy of the School of Visual Arts.

Agusta Agustsson, Polar Bear, Endangered. Silkscreen. 43" × 39". © The Graphic Workshop, Boston, MA 1980.

Creating Art

1. As a class, discuss some of the ways that graphic designers try to catch your attention. How could you use these methods in a poster of your own?

2. Think of a message you would like to communicate, or an idea, product, or interest you would like to advertise. You could make a poster for your favorite movie, TV show, book, or record. You could tell people about something that is important to you, or advertise a talent that you have. Draw your design on a large piece of paper and paint it with tempera paints. Your poster design should include words, and it should have a center of interest that will attract peoples' attention.

3. Display your poster in front of the class. Tell how you tried to think like a graphic designer as you created your artwork.

Art Materials	
Large white drawing paper	Mixing tray
	Water container
Pencil	Water, paper towels
Tempera paints	
Brush	Newspaper

Learning Outcomes

1. What are some important things a graphic designer must think about when planning a poster or other advertisement?

2. How did you create a center of interest in your poster?

3. What does graphic design contribute to our world? What are some examples of graphic design around you?

27 *Fill It with Patterns*

Observing and Thinking

Nature fills the world with **patterns**. **Textures**, **colors**, **lines**, and **shapes** all come together on natural things to form patterns. Stripes on zebras, shapes on turtles' shells, and scales on fish are all examples of natural patterns. Can you think of other animals or natural objects that have patterns?

Many of the patterns we see have their own kind of **rhythm**. One common kind of rhythm, or movement, that you will find in pattern is **repeating** rhythm. Repeating patterns are all the same, like a string of beads all the same size. **Alternating** patterns are like a string of beads with one small bead followed by a large one, then followed by a small one again, and so on. A **progressive** pattern has a rhythm that goes from small to larger, or from large to smaller.

Sometimes artists fill all the spaces on their pictures with patterns. They may use one or more types of rhythm in these patterns so that their pictures have variety and movement. Look for the alternating and repeating patterns in *Blue Clown—The Doorway* on page 59. What kinds of patterns are in the picture below by artist Jesse Allen?

Jesse Allen, Doe Stepping into the Afternoon. c. 1975. Etching. Courtesy of Vorpal Galleries: San Francisco and New York.

58

Paul Cline, Blue Clown—The Doorway. c. 1983. Acrylic on paper. 48″ × 72″. Courtesy of the artist.

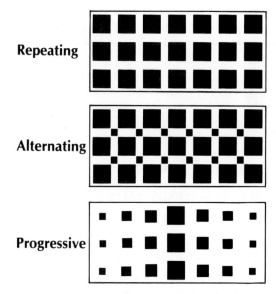

Repeating

Alternating

Progressive

Creating Art

1. On a small piece of white paper, draw a scene, person, animal, object, or design that has simple, basic shapes. Put several shapes in your picture, but keep the arrangement simple. You will be filling the shapes you draw, and the **negative spaces** between them, with patterns.

2. When you are satisfied with your design, start to fill in the shapes and the background spaces with rhythmic patterns. Use bright colored markers. Try different kinds of lines and shapes to fill the spaces with pattern. Make repeating, alternating, and progressive patterns.

Art Materials	
White drawing paper	Colored markers or crayons
Pencil	

Learning Outcomes

1. What are three types of rhythm you might find in patterns?

2. How did you fill your picture with pattern? What kinds of rhythm did you use?

3. Which of the pictures in this lesson shows the best use of pattern? What is the difference in the kinds of patterns you see?

28 Writing with Pictures

Observing and Thinking

Do you remember when you first learned the alphabet? You were learning that certain shapes were symbols for sounds, and that sounds put together made words.

Before alphabets were developed, people used pictures to communicate. They used **symbols** to represent objects and ideas.

Nootka Indian, Thunderbird and Killer Whale. *XIX Century. American Museum of National History.*

These symbols, or **pictographs**, were often simple and easy-to-recognize shapes. Some, though, were very detailed. The ancient Egyptians used a system of picture writing called **hieroglyphics**. Some of the Indian tribes of North and South America also used forms of picture writing. All of these people had their own special sets of symbols.

The Swiss artist Paul Klee was very interested in all forms of primitive art. In *Picture Album*, below, he used simple **lines** and **shapes** to make symbols that remind us of pictographs. What shapes can you identify? What do you think they symbolize? How did Klee achieve **rhythm** and **pattern**?

In this lesson, you will use **stencils** to create a symbolic design with simple shapes.

Paul Klee, Picture Album. *1937 ("Bilderbogen"). Gouache on unprimed canvas. 23⅜″ × 22¼″. The Phillips Collection, Washington, D.C.*

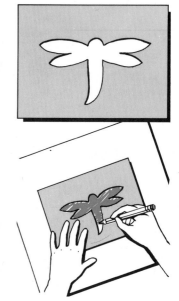

Egyptian, possibly from Assiut, Coffin of Khnumnakhte (detail: eye panel). *XII Dynasty, c. 1991-1786 B.C. Painted wood. 81.49"(l) × 20.47"(w) × 26.75"(h). The Metropolitan Museum of Art, Rogers Fund, 1915.*

Creating Art

1. Sketch several shapes that are symbols of objects or ideas important to you. These shapes can be **free-form** or **geometric**, **abstract** or **realistic**.

2. Make a stencil of each of your favorite symbols. Draw the symbol on a piece of thick paper or tagboard. Then carefully cut out the shape so that the outside part of the paper stays all in one piece. You will make three to five stencils in this way.

3. Use your finished stencils to make a pictograph design on your paper. Think carefully about where to place your shapes. With crayons or colored pencils, fill in the shapes of your stencils. Use several different colors. When you have made several stenciled shapes, look at your complete design.

4. When you have completed your stenciled design, you may want to add lines or other symbols to fill parts of the background, or negative, space. Think about how you can achieve rhythm and pattern in your design. When you are satisfied with your pictograph, pass it to a classmate. Discuss the message or story each pictograph tells.

Art Materials ◆ THINK SAFETY

Pencil	Scissors
Tagboard or heavy paper	Crayons, colored pencils, or oil pastels
White or light-colored drawing paper	

Learning Outcomes

1. What is a pictograph? Can you give some examples of pictographs?

2. Why did you select the symbols that you did? What do they stand for?

3. Tell how each work of art shown in the lesson uses symbols. What do you think the symbols mean?

29 *What Faces Say*

Observing and Thinking

Are you a "people-watcher"? Many artists are. They carefully observe people to see how they look and act. Some artists especially study people's faces. They know that a face can show deep emotions and tell about the character of a person. How can a face reveal a person's character or feelings?

Artists throughout history have made **portraits**, or images of people. The marble head of a Greek athlete shown to the right may or may not have been modeled from life. The person's uniqueness was not important.

Polykleitos, Statue of Diadoumenos: Roman copy of Greek original, detail (head, front). 440 B.C. Stone sculpture. The Metropolitan Museum of Art, Fletcher Fund, 1925. (25.78.56)

Joseph Turner Keiley, A Sioux Chief. ca. 1898. Glycerine developed platinum, mounted on gray paper with a narrow border upon a larger sheet of gray. 7⅝" × 5⁹⁄₁₆". The Metropolitan Museum of Art, The Alfred Stieglitz Collection, 1933.

Instead, the artist tried to express the ancient Greek **ideal** of peacefulness and calm. Compare this face to the photograph of a young Sioux Indian. What would you say about the character of this man? Does his face also express an ideal?

Since the invention of photography, artists have recorded the faces of people in real-life situations. Dorothea Lange's photograph of a poor woman during the Depression, shown on the next page, is a striking image of its time. What do you think this woman is feeling? What is happening in her life? How do her face and hands reveal her deep feelings? Can you give some reasons why this portrait is considered one of this century's greatest photographs?

Dorothea Lange, Migrant Mother,
California, 1936.

Creating Art

1. Spend some time studying photographs and artworks showing people's faces. Look through this book and other school books to find faces with interesting expressions. Act out different feelings with classmates and watch their expressions.

2. Make some quick sketches of faces showing various expressions. You may want to pair off with classmates and take turns modeling different expressions. From among your sketches, choose one that you would like to make into a finished portrait drawing. Draw the main shape of the head first so that it almost fills the paper. Then draw in the features, taking care to observe where they are placed. Human faces are **symmetrical** (sə-me′-tri-kəl), or the same on both sides. Eyes, nose, mouth, and ears are in the same relation, or **proportion**, to one another on every face. Yet, no two faces are exactly alike. Carefully observe the particular face you are drawing to discover its uniqueness.

Art Materials
White drawing paper	Pictures of faces
Pencil or charcoal	

Learning Outcomes

1. What are some of the things that faces can show?

2. What strong feeling did you show in your drawing of a face? How did you show it?

3. Which face on these pages shows the strongest emotion? Why do you say so?

30 The Wild Beasts

Observing and Thinking

Some artists paint things in colors that you would not expect to see. They use color in unrealistic ways. Study the painting on this page. What colors did Henri Matisse use to paint this picture of a girl reading? What is unusual about these colors? Why do you think Matisse used them?

A group of French artists started to use intense and unexpected colors in their work in the early 1900s. Because of the bold, almost violent colors they used, they were called the **Fauves** (fōhvz), which is French for "wild beasts." Matisse was the leader of this **movement**, or trend, in art. He and other artists used color and rapid, energetic brushstrokes to express emotion or to show **emphasis** in parts of their paintings.

The Fauves' use of color greatly influenced later artists. Andy Warhol was a well-known artist of the 1960s. He silk-screened his **self-portrait** six times, using unusual color combinations in each. Which color combination do you think is the most realistic in his portrait on page 65? Which is the least?

Henri Matisse, Girl Reading (La Lecture). Winter 1905–06. Oil on canvas. 28⅝″ × 23⅜″. Collection, Mr. and Mrs. David Rockefeller.

Andy Warhol, Self-Portrait. 1966. Synthetic polymer paint and enamel silk-screened on six canvases, each 22⅝" × 22⅝". The Sidney and Harriet Janis Collection. Gift to the Museum of Modern Art, New York.

Creating Art

1. On a piece of paper, sketch the outline of your face or the face of a model. Add the features: the eyes, nose, and mouth. Your pencil lines should be very, very light so that you can barely see them. Observe your own face or your model's carefully as you draw.

2. Follow the pencil lines so that you know where to paint the parts of the face. Use unusual and unexpected colors as you paint. Mix bright and bold colors that you would never see in a person's real face and hair. Your paint should be thick.

3. As you paint, let your paints mix together on the paper in places. Paint in a background. Use bright colors, lines, and patterns in the background of your painting.

Art Materials	
White paper	Brush
Pencil	Water container
Tempera paints	Water, paper towels
Mixing tray	
Mirror (optional)	Newspapers

Learning Outcomes

1. How did the Fauves use color? What effects were they trying to achieve?

2. How did you use colors in unusual and unexpected ways?

3. Which of the paintings shown here tells more about the person in the painting? Why do you think so?

65

31 The Peaceable Kingdom

Observing and Thinking

Can you think of some subjects, or **themes**, that you see over and over again in works of art? Some of the great themes of art include such subjects as people at work and at play, the world of nature, dreams and fantasy, and war and peace. Different artists will treat the same theme in different ways.

See how three different artists painted the theme of the peaceable kingdom. The peaceable kingdom is a world of perfect peace. Animals who would normally be enemies are shown living together in harmony. What other **symbols** of peace do you see in these paintings?

The paintings shown here are examples of primitive art. Primitive artists are self-taught artists who have had little or no training in the **techniques** of art. They paint simply for their own and other people's enjoyment.

Edward Hicks, an American artist, painted over one hundred versions, or **variations**, of his painting, *The Peaceable Kingdom.* Horace Pippin, a black American artist, painted his own versions of the theme. He made some of America's finest primitive paintings. Gustavo Novoa is a **contemporary** artist from Chile who paints in a primitive **style**. He paints jungle creatures who represent a perfect world of love and peace. What qualities make his painting seem peaceful?

Horace Pippin, Holy Mountain III. 1945. Oil on canvas. 25¼" × 30¼". Hirshhorn Museum and Sculpture Garden, Smithsonian Institution.

Edward Hicks, The Peaceable Kingdom. *Oil on canvas. 44.5″ × 60.2″. Worcester Art Museum.*

Gustavo Novoa, Suburbia. *Reproduced with permission of Gustavo Novoa. Represented by Wally Findlay Galleries, U.S.A.*

Creating Art

1. Study the paintings by Pippin, Hicks, and Novoa. Are their paintings realistic? How are the animals like real animals? How are they different?

2. Imagine a world of perfect peace. What will the setting be like? What kinds of animals would you put together to show that there is harmony in this world? Will you include people? What colors will you use to show peace? When you have a clear idea of your world of peace in your mind, draw it on paper. Fill the entire page with your drawing. Don't worry about making your art look realistic. The important thing is the feeling you put into your painting. What will be the **center of interest** in your work? How will you show it?

3. Paint your picture with thick tempera paints. When your picture is dry, display it with the other pictures from your class.

Art Materials	
White drawing paper	Mixing tray
Pencil	Water, paper towels
Tempera paints	Water container
Brush	Newspaper

Learning Outcomes

1. What is a theme? Name some themes used often in works of art.

2. What did you include in your painting to show peace? Did you use any symbols of peace, or symbolic colors?

3. Which version of the peaceable kingdom theme do you like best? Why?

Exploring Art

A Classroom Mural

Are there any murals in your community? A **mural** is a picture or design that decorates an inside or outside wall. Most murals are painted directly onto the surface of a wall. Some are painted onto canvas or another material and later attached to a wall.

Mural art is one of the oldest forms of **decoration**. Even the cavemen painted their cave walls with pictures of the animals they hunted. The ancient Egyptians painted the insides of tomb walls with scenes that showed what had been important to the people buried there. The Romans decorated the walls of their homes with landscape scenes and pictures of the gods and goddesses they worshipped. Today, in America, murals are often a very important form of city, or *urban*, art. Murals are often painted in public places to reflect the values and concerns of the community.

You may think of art as something that you do by yourself. Yet, the creation of a mural can allow many people to work together to produce a work of art. Your entire class can work together to create a school or classroom mural. How will you begin? Making a classroom mural will take some decision-making on your part. What will each student's contribution be? What subject will you choose to paint? How can you create a unified **composition** when so many different people are involved in the effort? A mural project can be a challenging, fun experience for the entire class.

Review

Using What You Have Learned

American artist Edward Hopper painted many scenes of New York City and small towns in New England. He showed the ordinary scenes and objects of daily life: service stations, diners, hotels, shops, and streets. Hopper often seemed to freeze a single moment in time. He used colors that express a moody feeling. Many of his paintings show great empty spaces that add to his repeated **theme** of loneliness. Study *Cape Cod Evening,* keeping in mind some of the things you have learned about art.

Edward Hopper, Cape Cod Evening. 1939. Oil on canvas. 30¼" × 40¼".
National Gallery of Art, Washington, D.C. John Hay Whitney Collection.

1. What is the mood of this painting? How did Hopper create this mood?

2. What is the **center of interest** in this painting? What leads your eyes to this center of interest?

3. What colors did Hopper use? Can you find **warm** or **cool colors**? **Tints** or **shades**? **Analogous** or **complementary** colors? **Neutral** colors? Why do you think that Hopper made some of these color choices in this painting?

4. How did Edward Hopper achieve **unity** in this work of art?

5. What kinds of brushstrokes did Hopper use in this painting?

6. What kind of **balance** is shown in the **composition** of this painting? What is the effect of this balance?

7. What do you think is happening in this painting? How does Hopper make you wonder about what is going on?

Unit 3

Thinking Like an Artist

Michael A. Naranjo, The Bath.
Bronze. Edition: 2. Female figure:
63" high; child figure: 21" high.
Courtesy of Michael and Laurie
Naranjo, Espanola, New Mexico.

Art is like a problem with no one correct answer. Every work of art you create involves some kind of problem-solving. As you have worked through the lessons in this book, you have learned more about how to see like an artist. You have also learned more about the many different purposes people have in creating art. You have come to understand that art is more than observing, imagining, and expressing. It is also hard work, requiring a knowledge of the tools, materials, and techniques artists use.

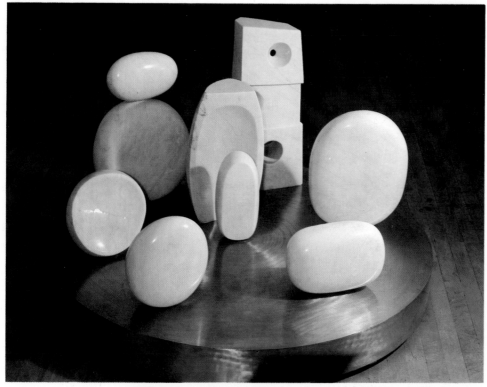

Barbara Hepworth, Assembly of Sea Forms. *1972. White marble. 8 pcs. mounted on revolving stainless steel plinth. Norton Simon Art Foundation.*

As you learn more about various art forms, you learn that some **media** are more suited to certain types of artistic expression than others. You learn that there are limits to what you can do in some media, and that these limits force you to think through problems in self-expression through art. The more you learn about handling different media, the better you will be able to choose the best form for the art you want to create.

Many people find that they prefer certain media, techniques, or tools over others after they have experimented with different kinds of art. Sometimes they develop strengths in certain types of art. They may even decide to make a **career** out of the kind of art they do best, whether it is sculpture, commercial art, painting, weaving, or crafts work. Is there one kind of art that you prefer over others?

In this unit, you will learn more about **three-dimensional** art forms. You will also learn various techniques for improving two-dimensional artwork so that it seems to have three-dimensional depth. You will have a

chance to work with different art forms, such as sculpture, jewelry-making, and papier-mâché. The more you learn about different media, the better you will be able to choose the medium that is best for expressing your artistic ideas. And the better you will be able to appreciate all the many kinds of art that you can find in the world around you.

32 The Illusion of Depth

Observing and Thinking

Have you ever seen drawings or paintings that looked as though you could step right into them? When artists work on a flat, or **two-dimensional**, surface, they often try to create **perspective**, the illusion of depth and distance. The proper use of perspective makes a flat work appear **three-dimensional**.

Artists try to achieve perspective in various ways. If you study the photograph of Picasso holding an umbrella, you will see what three of these ways are. Why does the woman appear larger than Picasso and the man behind him? What is the effect of her arm **overlapping** part of Picasso's figure? Why does the last man's body appear to be farther up from the bottom of the page? Why does he appear to be smaller than Picasso?

In drawings and paintings, artists show objects that are closer by making them larger and nearer to the bottom of the page than the other objects. Objects that are farther away will appear smaller and higher up on the page. They may also be overlapped by objects that are in front of them. Why couldn't the closest object be overlapped by something?

Tell how the photograph of Picasso and his friends shows all three ways of achieving perspective. Do you see any of these same methods used in the **still life** painting by Tom Wesselman on page 73?

In this lesson, you will arrange a still life picture of various foods, showing the illusion of depth in two or more ways.

Pablo Picasso on the beach with Françoise Gilot.
Photograph by Robert Capa.

Tom Wesselman, Still Life No. 25. 1963. Oil and assemblage on composition board. 48″ × 72″ × 4″. Rose Art Museum, Brandeis University, Waltham, Massachusetts. Gevirtz-Mnuchin Purchase Fund.

Creating Art

1. Draw a picture of a fruit, vegetable, or other food item twice. You may work from **models** of actual foods. The first drawing should be large. The second drawing should be smaller. Choose several other food items, and draw two versions of each: one large and one small.

2. Look at the food items you have drawn and choose the three large/small pairs that you like best. Cut out these drawings. Arrange them on a background of colored paper. How can you show the parts of the picture that are farthest away? How can you show the parts that are closest?

3. Arrange the parts of your still life several times before you paste them down. Make sure that you show an arrangement that is balanced. If you like, go over the lines of your drawn food objects with a black marker and add color.

Art Materials

THINK SAFETY

White paper

Colored paper

Pencil

Colored markers

Scissors

Paste

Crayons

Food items for models

Learning Outcomes

1. What three ways can artists use to make objects look closer or farther away?

2. How did you arrange the objects in your still life so that they showed the illusion of depth, or perspective?

3. Compare the photograph of Picasso and his friends with the still life by Tom Wesselman. Which one shows the illusion of depth most convincingly?

33 More About Depth and Distance

Observing and Thinking

When a flat picture appears to have depth and distance, we say that it shows **perspective**. Study the painting called *Pilgrims Going to Church*, shown below. Do you see that the picture has three different parts, or levels? In the closest part of the picture there are three trees, a rock, and a tree stump. Artists call this the **foreground** of the picture. The pilgrims walking in a group are in the middle part, or **middleground**, of the picture. They are walking on a winding path towards the building and trees that are in the **background** of the picture. Why do these parts of the picture appear smaller than the parts in the foreground or middleground?

Look at the far right-hand side of the painting. The artist has painted a man near the end of the group. Notice how much smaller he appears than the other people in the group. Is this man closer to or farther away from the foreground than the rest of the pilgrims? Notice how the rest of the people are placed in the picture. Are their feet all touching the same level of ground? How does this add to the illusion of depth? Does this painting show perspective successfully?

George H. Boughton, Pilgrims Going to Church. *Courtesy of The New York Historical Society, New York.*

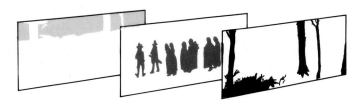

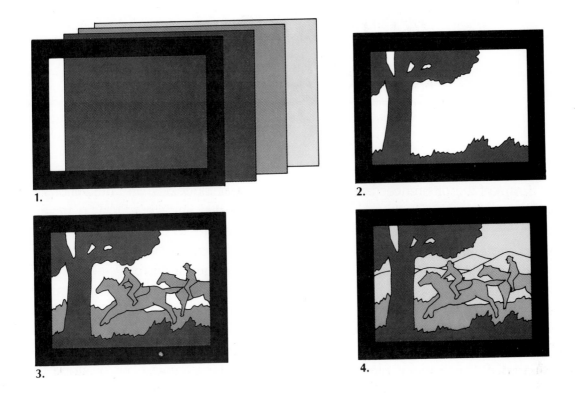

1.

2.

3.

4.

Creating Art

1. Cut out the middle of a piece of black construction paper, leaving a two-inch border all the way around. You have made a **mat**, or frame, of your black paper.

2. Use your smallest-length sheet of paper to draw objects for the foreground of your picture. You could include rocks, trees, bushes, or even people. The "ground" part of your foreground should be at least two-and-a-half inches high so that it will peek up from the bottom of the mat. Color your foreground. Cut it out, and attach it to the back of your mat.

3. Use your medium-sized piece of paper for the middleground. Draw the objects of your middleground at least two-and-a-half inches or more from the bottom of your paper. Then color your middleground, and cut away the "sky" part carefully.

   Attach your middleground to the edges of the back of your mat with tagboard strips. Your middleground will curve out in back a little.

4. Use your longest piece of paper for the background. The objects in the background will appear smaller than other objects in your picture. Why? Color your background, and attach it to the edges of your mat so that it curves out in back.

Art Materials

THINK SAFETY

Black construction paper   Scissors

White drawing paper   Stapler

    Pencil

Tagboard strips   Crayons

Learning Outcomes

1. What are some ways that an artist can show perspective in a scene?

2. How did you show distance in the three levels of your picture?

3. Look through this book for other paintings that show perspective. Which paintings use perspective most effectively?

34 All About Relief Sculpture

Observing and Thinking

What are some of the differences between a drawing and a sculpture? The biggest difference, of course, is that a drawing is flat and **two-dimensional**, while a sculpture is solid and **three-dimensional**. But there is a type of sculpture that has qualities of both these art forms. It is called **relief sculpture**.

Relief sculpture has areas that are raised out from a flat background surface. The shapes of a relief sculpture are either carved out of the surface, built up by adding bits of clay, or cut out separately and added on to a flat surface. Some relief surfaces are made by molds, too. You see relief surfaces every day: just look at the coins in your pocket. Jewelry,

fancy belt buckles, and medallions also often have relief surfaces. Do you have a medal, plaque, or wall decoration at home that is an example of a relief?

Throughout history, relief sculpture has been used to decorate doors, buildings, and walls. Many relief sculptures in the ancient world told stories, showing figures of men and animals in action poses. Because these reliefs were carved out of stone or marble, they have lasted for thousands of years. But reliefs can be made of other materials, too, such as wood, metal, ivory, or clay.

In this lesson, you will make your own relief sculpture out of clay.

Victor Schreckengost, Mammoths. c. 1955. Terra-cotta mural from the Pachyderm Building, Cleveland Metroparks Zoo.

76

Egypt, Sculptor's model or trial piece. Late Dynastic or Early Ptolemaic. 6⁷⁄₁₀″ × 7²⁄₅″. The Metropolitan Museum of Art. Gift of Edward S. Harkness, 1917–1918.

Evelyn Ackerman, Animal Blocks. c. 1971. Carved in clear all-heart redwood. Small blocks 9½″ square; large blocks 19″ × 9½″. Manufactured by Era Industries. Copyright © Forms and Surfaces. Courtesy of Evelyn Ackerman.

Creating Art

1. Use a rolling pin to make a clay slab of an even thickness. Cut the clay into a large geometric shape of your choice, using an old table knife or Popsicle stick. You can make a medallion or a plaque, if you wish. If you want a round shape, use a coffee can lid as your guide. Save the clay you cut off.

2. Smooth water around the edges of your clay. With a pencil, scratch in a picture of the subject of your relief sculpture. It can be an animal, a person's head, a scene with buildings, a landscape, or whatever you like.

3. Dig out the clay around the shape, forming the flat background. The more you dig out around the shape, the more raised your relief will be. Use a Popsicle stick, paperclips, or other tools to dig out the background. Even your fingers will do!

4. When you have made all the main parts of your subject and dug out enough of the background, smooth and model the shapes carefully so that they look as though they rise smoothly from the background. If you wish, you may use drinking straws, natural objects, forks, or whatever you like to make **textures** on the surface of the relief.

5. Poke two holes near the top of the slab with a straw if you want to hang your relief on a wall later.

Art Materials	THINK SAFETY
Water-based clay	Paper towels
Rolling pin	Pencil
Water	Carving tools
Water container	Drinking straw
Newspaper	

Learning Outcomes

1. How is relief sculpture like a "halfway" form between drawing and sculpture?

2. How did you create interest in your relief sculpture by carving out the background and adding textures?

3. How many examples of relief sculpture can you find in your environment?

77

35 *Stylized Animal Shapes*

Observing and Thinking

If you wanted to show an animal in art, what **medium**, or material, would you use? You could paint it, showing its colors and patterns. You could make a pencil drawing, using shading to show its solid **form** and the texture of its fur, hair, or feathers. You could even make a **sculpture** of the animal, showing how it looks in three dimensions.

Artists who work in the medium of **sculpture** have several choices of the types of sculptures they may make. One of the oldest forms of three-dimensional art is **carving**, a type of **subtractive sculpture**. In subtractive sculpture, the artist subtracts, or takes away from, the material he or she started with.

When carving, the artist uses various tools to carefully cut away parts of stone, ivory, bone, wood, or other materials to reveal a form.

Carving produces smooth forms with flowing lines. Details and textures are often not very important in carving, so carvings may show **stylized** shapes that represent something in a simplified way. Can you name some subjects that would be especially suited to the medium of carving?

Study the animal carvings in this lesson. How did each artist use the unique qualities of carving to create a successful work of art? In this lesson, you will create your own stylized carving of an animal.

François Pompon, Polar Bear. White marble on black marble base. 9⅜" × 19". The Metropolitan Museum of Art. Gift of Edward C. Moore, Jr., 1930. (30.123ab)

John B. Flannagan, Chimpanzee. 1928. Granite. 10¾"(h) × 8"(w) × 6¾"(d). Collection of Whitney Museum of American Art, New York.

Alaskan Eskimo, Walrus. 19th century. William Hammond Mathers Museum at Indiana University. Acc. No. 57-1-425

Creating Art

1. Draw a few simple sketches showing the **main shape** of an animal that you would like to carve. Remember that you will not be carving lots of details and textures into your sculpture. Concentrate on making the shape of the animal simple.

2. Model a lump of clay into the basic position you want your animal to be: standing or lying down. When you have made your basic animal shape, start to carve it. Use tools such as Popsicle sticks, large paper clips, and plastic knives to take away parts of the clay, gradually revealing the form of your animal. As you work, keep turning the clay so that you can get a good view of each side of the sculpture.

3. Remember to dip your fingers in water and gently rub the surface of the clay to keep it smooth and free of cracks. Carve simple shapes that have gently curving lines to create your animal forms. Have you captured the special qualities of the animal you carved?

Art Materials

Drawing paper	Water container
Pencil	Carving tools
Clay	Newspaper
Water	Paper towels

THINK SAFETY

Learning Outcomes

1. What is subtractive sculpture? Can you name one type of subtractive sculpture?

2. How did you make your animal shape simple, or stylized?

3. How can artists capture the special qualities of a subject without using a lot of textures or details?

79

36 Body Language

Observing and Thinking

If you couldn't see a person's face, could you tell what he or she was feeling? People's faces may be hidden, yet their bodies can still give messages about what they are really feeling. This kind of visual communication is called "body language."

Study the artworks in this lesson. *Family Group* by American painter William Glackens shows four figures whose postures reveal much more than their faces do. What do you think these people feel about each other? What can you tell about these people just by observing their body language?

Despair by Hugo Robus says it all in its title. This sculpture is an **abstract** form of a person. Yet, it is full of emotion. How did the sculptor capture such powerful feelings without showing a lot of detail?

Thomas Eakins seems to be peeking in on *Miss Van Buren* in an unguarded moment. Do you think she knows that anyone is watching her? What might she be feeling? What thoughts do you think are running through her mind? Why do you say so?

In this lesson, you will study body language by drawing from a live model.

William Glackens, Family Group. 1910-1911. Canvas. 72" × 84".
National Gallery of Art, Washington, D.C. Gift of Mr. and Mrs. Ira Glackens.

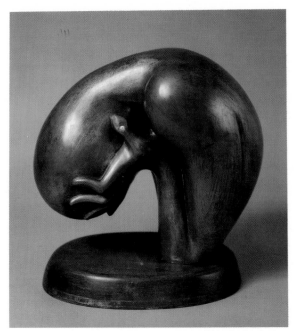

Hugo Robus, Despair. 1927. Bronze. 12¾″ × 10″ × 13″. Collection of Whitney Museum of American Art.

Thomas Eakins, Miss Van Buren. c. 1886-1890. Oil on canvas. 44½″ × 32″. The Phillips Collection, Washington, D.C.

Creating Art

1. Watch as your model goes through several poses that illustrate body language. Ask your model to express anger, fear, and joy with his or her body. Think of any other emotions that can be expressed without words or even facial expressions.

2. When your model has taken a pose that you like, do several quick sketches. Look closely at the model and at the paper. Look back and forth between your paper and the model so that you can draw the position of the head, the way the arms and shoulders are held, and the posture of the entire body.

3. Look over your sketches. Which one do you like best? Choose a sketch, and draw over it with a black marker to make a finished drawing. Add details. Show what the model is wearing. Also show some of the surroundings—the floor and any objects around the model. Color your finished drawing, if you wish.

Art Materials	
White drawing paper	Model
	Black felt marker
Pencil	Crayons or paints

Learning Outcomes

1. What is body language? What clues did you find in the pictures in this lesson that told you what the people were feeling?

2. What kind of feeling did you try to show in your picture? How did you show it?

3. Which of the artworks in the lesson do you think shows the most emotion through body language?

37 *Sports Heroes*

Observing and Thinking

Artists since ancient times have used athletes as **images** in art. Sometimes the athletes are shown in action, as in the painting, *The Football Player*. Other artworks show figures just before the moment of action, as in Thomas Eakins' painting of baseball players. We can see the movement of the football player. How are tension and a sense of movement created in the picture of the baseball players?

Artists often show sports heroes exactly as they are. They make them look **realistic**. Many times, though, artists will show simplified or **abstract** forms of athletes. An abstract figure of an athlete will focus on the simple shapes and movements of the figure. Which of the two paintings shown here is more realistic? Which is more abstract?

Artists are interested in creating **unity** in their work. They may do this by limiting the number of objects or people shown in a picture. Another way to develop unity is to have figures that touch or **overlap** each other. Do you see either technique used in these paintings? Give an example of each.

In this lesson, you will create a unified picture of sports heroes that uses both realistic and abstract figures.

Francoise Gilot, The Football Player. *1974. Oil. 32" × 39½". Courtesy of Riggs Galleries, San Diego. Copyright © 1974 Françoise Gilot.*

82

Thomas Eakins, Baseball Players Practicing. 1875. Watercolor. Museum of Art, Rhode Island School of Design. Jesse Metcalf Fund and Walter H. Kimball Fund.

Creating Art

1. Decide on a sports figure you would like to draw. Use a pencil to sketch the figure in action. The figure should be five or six inches high. You may use a photograph to see what the athlete looks like. Do not trace the photograph, but draw what you see, making your picture realistic.

2. When you are satisfied with your drawing, color it with crayons. Make the skin tones and other colors as realistic as possible.

3. Cut out the figure. Now outline this cutout shape three times on a piece of paper, creating **silhouettes**. Overlap the shapes to create a sense of motion and action. You can use your paper in either a horizontal or vertical position.

4. Use crayons to color the overlapping outline shapes. Use bright, solid colors.

5. Paint a watercolor **wash** over the paper. Wet the entire paper and brush on two or three colors so that they run together. The crayon-colored shapes will stand out. This is called a **crayon resist**, because the

watercolor wash will not stick to the waxy crayon surface.

6. When the paint is dry, the realistic cutout of the sports figure can be pasted into the composition where it looks best.

Art Materials	THINK SAFETY
White paper	Watercolors
Photographs of sports figures (from magazines)	Brush
	Water container
Pencil	Paper towels
Crayons	Newspaper
Scissors	Paste

Learning Outcomes

1. What are two ways that artists can create unity in their artwork?

2. How did you develop unity in your own sports design?

3. Explain how Gilot and Eakins achieved unity in their paintings.

38 Modeling Figures in Clay

Observing and Thinking

Do you enjoy working with clay? Clay can be a marvelous **medium** to use because it fully involves your sense of touch. As you roll clay in your hands, feeling it between your fingers, you can often get ideas for a **form** you can shape. You might start to model a person, and end up with a strange-looking creature from your imagination instead.

Clay is fun to use, and you can usually correct mistakes easily. Like every other medium, though, there are limits to what you can do with clay. If you make clay parts that are too thin and stick out from the main part of the clay, they will fall off or droop. That is why it is hard to model standing people or animal figures out of clay. When artists make clay models of sculptures they plan to carve or mold, they often use a wire skeleton, called an **armature**, inside the clay. In this way, they can build up clay around the armature so that it stays up to form figures with arms and legs that won't droop or collapse.

Look at the sculptures shown in this lesson. Do you think that an armature was used in any of them? Could any of them be made without an armature? Why or why not?

In this lesson, you will model a person, animal, or fantasy creature out of clay. Since you will not be using an armature, your clay figure's body parts must lie close to the body.

David Gilhooly, Merfrog and Her Pet Fish. 1976. Glazed ceramic. 42" × 29" × 48". Collection of Whitney Museum of American Art. Gift of Mr. and Mrs. William A. Marsteller, the John I.H. Baur Purchase Fund (and purchase). Acq. #79.26

Japanese, Haniwa Horse. III-VI Centuries. Terra cotta. 23½" × 26". The Cleveland Museum of Art, The Norweb Collection.

Creating Art

1. There are several ways to model a figure out of clay. You can start with a single lump of clay and form it into the basic shape you want. Then you can make arms, legs, and other features that lie close to the body. You can also start with a single piece of clay and add on **coils**, or rolls, of clay to form arms, legs, and other body parts. You can attach these parts with a mixture of clay, vinegar, and water called **slip**.

2. Decide what position your figure will be: standing, sitting, or lying down. It will be easier for you to model a figure in which body parts lie close to the main part of the body, as you see in the sculpture of Mer-frog by David Gilhooly.

3. Pinch, bend, and smooth your clay to form the parts of the figure. When you are satisfied with the shape and position of your figure, start to add details. Use forks, toothpicks, paper clips, and textured objects to make interesting textures. Use thin strands of clay to make hair.

4. As you work, keep turning your clay figure so that you can see how it looks from all sides. Your figure can be serious, scary, or silly, but it should be original.

Art Materials

Water-based clay	Paper towels
Water	Objects for making textures
Water container	
Newspapers	

Learning Outcomes

1. What is an armature? When would a clay sculptor need to use one?

2. Did you plan out the figure you made, or let it form itself as you worked? How did you make textures in your clay surface?

3. Which of the sculptures shown in this lesson looks most carefully planned? Which looks as though the artist created it as he or she went along?

39 Can You Tell What It Is?

Observing and Thinking

Can you recognize what each sculpture on this page is? How have the artists changed these forms so that they no longer look exactly like real people or animals?

When artists **simplify** forms, we say that they make them **abstract**. We can still recognize the objects or figures in abstract art, but they have been changed to make them more interesting or to express the artist's ideas.

Pablo Picasso made many abstract figures by simplifying forms. Sometimes he **exaggerated** qualities. How did he exaggerate goatlike qualities in the sculpture below?

Alberto Giacometti (jäk-ə-met'-ē) made many long, stick-like sculptures of people. He thought that people were separated from one another even though they lived in crowded cities. He **distorted** human figures on purpose to express his ideas about loneliness.

The *Cycladic Figure* is also a **stylized**, or simplified, form. We recognize it as human, but it is abstract rather than **realistic**. When would you guess it was carved? If you said over 4,000 years ago, you guessed right! Many people think it looks modern because the form is very abstract.

Pablo Picasso, She-Goat. 1950. Bronze (cast 1952), after found objects. 46⅜" × 56⅜", base 41⅛" × 28⅛". Collection, The Museum of Modern Art, New York. Mrs. Simon Guggenheim Fund.

Alberto Giacometti, Man Pointing. 1947. Bronze. 70½" high, at base 12" × 13¼". Collection, The Museum of Modern Art, New York. Gift of Mrs. John D. Rockefeller 3rd.

Greece, Keros-Syros Culture, Cycladic Figure. 2200–2000 B.C. Marble. 34½". Los Angeles County Museum of Art. Gift of Anna Bing Arnold.

3. Strengthen the arms and legs by molding them firmly. If you didn't mold a head from the body, attach one with T-pins. Other body parts may be added in the same way. What have you made? Can you tell what it is?

Art Materials
Heavy-duty aluminum foil   Masking tape
Scissors   Large T-pins (optional)

Creating Art

1. Start with a large square or rectangular piece of aluminum foil. Roll four smaller pieces to form the "arms" and/or "legs" of your abstract sculpture. Attach them with masking tape to the non-shiny side of your aluminum foil sheet, as in the photograph on page 86.

2. Carefully fold and mold the "body" around the arms and legs. As you work, let the form suggest ideas to you. If your sheet is large enough, you may be able to mold a head and neck from the body.

Learning Outcomes

1. Explain what *abstract* means.

2. In what ways is your sculpture an abstract form of the real thing?

3. What thoughts or feelings do you think are being expressed in each of the sculptures shown here?

40 Building Shapes

Observing and Thinking

What shapes are the walls of your classroom? What shapes make up the outside of the building? What shapes do you see in the roof? In the floor?

Buildings are usually made up of **geometric shapes**, such as squares and rectangles, that are put together to make cubes and boxes. The angles that we see are 90° or *right angles.* These are the shapes and angles that we are most familiar with and see in our homes, schools, and other public places.

Some of today's **architects** like to use other kinds of shapes and angles in their buildings. Sometimes, as in the Annapolis Federal Savings and Loan Building, shown below, architects introduce shapes that are meant to remind people of something else. Do you see the triangular shapes that look like sails? Annapolis is the home of the Naval Academy, and boats have sailed up the river to dock at this town for many years.

A well-known architect named R. Buckminster Fuller made buildings that were shaped like **spheres**, or round balls. People sometimes called these buildings "Bucky's Bubbles," but they are really **geodesic** (jē-ə-des'-ik) **domes**. Look at the geodesic dome shown below. Can you identify the smaller shapes that make up the frame of the dome?

In this lesson, you will use various shapes to make a model building that looks like no other building you have ever seen.

R. Buckminster Fuller, Geodesic Dome. *Montreal, Canada.*

Annapolis Federal Savings and Loan Building, Annapolis, Maryland.

Eero Saarinen, David S. Ingalls Hockey Rink at Yale University, *New Haven, Connecticut. Courtesy of Yale Sports Information.*

Creating Art

1. Think about what shapes you want to use in your building. You will need to plan how the shapes will go together to create space inside the building. You will also need to think about the **purpose** of your building and plan the shapes and spaces so that they are functional.

2. Cut shapes out of heavy white paper or thin cardboard. As you cut, you may want to leave tabs or ways to join the shapes together. You may also want to cut out spaces for windows. Paste the shapes together. You may need to use paper clips or tape temporarily until the paste dries.

3. Cut out a human figure and attach it near your model to show the **scale**, or size, of the building. Write a description that tells the shapes you used, why you used them, and the purpose of the building.

Art Materials	
Heavy white paper	Ruler
Thin white cardboard	Paper clips
Pencil	Objects to add to make details on the model
Scissors	
Paste	Tape

Learning Outcomes

1. What shapes and angles do architects commonly use in designing buildings?

2. How did you decide on the shapes you used in your model?

3. What shapes were used to make the buildings shown in this lesson? What other kinds of shapes could an architect use in a building?

41 Hand-Built Pottery

Observing and Thinking

Have you ever seen a pottery maker, or **potter**, at work? Since ancient times, much pottery has been made using a device called a **potter's wheel**. The wheel helps the potter to make a perfectly shaped piece of pottery from soft clay. Yet pottery can also be "hand-built," or shaped entirely by hand.

There are several different ways to make pottery by hand. You know, from working with clay, that it is easy to form it into shapes. One way that you can form pottery into shapes is by the **pinch method**. Start with a lump of clay and form it into a ball shape. Then press your thumb into the clay. Squeeze the clay between your thumb and index finger, working the clay outward from the bottom up. Turn the ball of clay as you work so that you can make a clay form that looks good from all sides.

Another common method of hand-building is the **slab method**. Roll clay into a flat slab. Cut shapes from the slab and join them together with a creamy mixture of water, clay, and vinegar called **slip**.

Look at the pottery pieces shown below. They are from different cultures and times. Which hand-building method could be used to make such shapes?

In this lesson, you will "hand-build" clay to make a piece of pottery that you can use.

Acoma Indians of New Mexico, Water Jar with Parrot Motif. *1885. National Museum of Natural History, Smithsonian Institution, Washington, D.C.*

Iran, Jar, decorated with three-horned animals between geometric designs. Prehistoric period, ca. 3400 B.C.. Pottery, unglazed. 20⅞"(h) × 19⅛"(d). The Metropolitan Museum of Art. Purchase, 1959, Joseph Pulitzer Bequest.

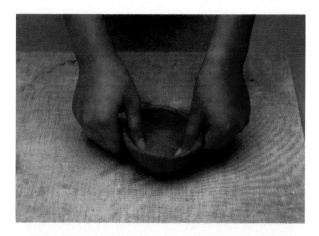

Creating Art

1. Think about a piece of pottery that you would like to make. What method could you use to make it: pinch or slab? When you decide on the best method, take a lump of clay and start to work with it.

2. Some artists like to form the clay in their hands with no real idea of what the pottery will end up looking like. Don't be afraid to experiment with your clay. Your piece does not have to look like a perfect example from a potter's wheel. Sometimes the handmade imperfections in a piece of pottery make it more interesting.

3. When you have made your basic shape, you may want to add **texture** to the surface using such tools as forks, paperclips, combs, found objects, and so on.

Art Materials

Clay	Tools for making textures
Water, paper towels	Rolling pin (optional)
Water container	
Newspaper	

Learning Outcomes

1. Describe two methods for "hand-building" pottery.

2. Which method did you use to create your piece of pottery?

3. What do you think might have been the function of each pottery piece shown in this lesson? Why do you say so?

42 *Colorful Mexican Folk Art*

Observing and Thinking

If you ever visit a village market in Mexico, you will see a world of excitement and color. Handmade crafts abound in Mexico. Everything, from clothing and pottery to toys and rugs, is made in sunny, pure colors.

The Mexican people have a long tradition of handmade crafts, or **handicrafts**. These handicrafts are among the most beautiful and interesting examples of world **folk art**. For generations, the Mexican people have handed down the knowledge of how to make everyday items, such as pottery, dresses, hats, baskets, boxes, bowls, and a thousand other useful items. Sometimes a certain village may be known for one kind of craft, such as weaving, mask-making, copperwork, basketry, or pottery-making.

Most of the objects that Mexican craftworkers create are made to serve particular functions. Yet, beauty is as important as usefulness to the Mexican people. They express their views of life in the bright colors and decorations they choose to use in their crafts. The world of fantasy and the imagination is very important to the Mexican people. From toys to baskets, the handicrafts of Mexico show a sense of fun, a respect for the natural world, and a colorful zest for life.

In this lesson, you will create a colorful creature inspired by the qualities of Mexican folk art. You will make your creature out of **papier-mâché**, a method of sculpting using newspaper and a special paste mixture.

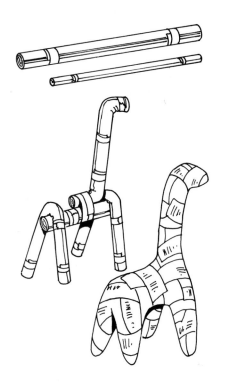

Creating Art

1. First, create a skeleton, or **armature**, for the creature you want to make. Use rolls of newspaper to make the body, legs, and head, as shown in the illustration. You may make a **stylized** shape of a common animal, such as an elephant or horse, or make a fantasy creature. You can make an animal that is sitting down or standing up. Tape the parts of the body together.

2. When your armature is completed, you can adjust the position of the animal. Tape on wads of crumpled paper to make the body fatter in parts, if you need to.

3. Tear strips of newspaper and dip them one at a time into your paste mixture. Cover the creature's entire body, adding only a layer at a time. Build up your figure so that it starts to take on the form you want. You can add final details like large ears that stick out, a tail, a fin on the back, or whatever you like.

4. When papier-mâché is dry, it becomes very strong and hard. Paint it, using bright tempera paints. Mexican artists use colors like bright blue, yellow, violet, green, pink, red, orange, and black. When the first coat of paint is dry, you may add details, such as flower designs or strange patterns.

Art Materials		THINK SAFETY
Newspapers	Plastic containers	
Tape	Water, paper towels	
Scissors	Tempera paints	
Papier-mâché paste	Brushes	

Learning Outcomes

1. What are some of the qualities of Mexican folk art?

2. What kind of a creature did you create? What qualities of Mexican folk art did you use in your artwork?

3. How do Mexican folk artists make the objects they create both beautiful and functional?

93

43 Pinning It On

Observing and Thinking

People have always liked to wear things that make them look more attractive. Jewelry is one of the many decorative articles that a person might wear for **adornment**. Do you wear any kinds of jewelry? Before you answer, consider all the types of jewelry there are. Not all jewelry is made for decorative purposes. Some jewelry, such as wristwatches, serves a practical function as well. Medical bracelets, metal identification tags, medals that honor athletes and heroes, good-luck charms, and pins with messages are all types of jewelry. What other kinds of jewelry can you name?

For centuries, jewelry was worn by powerful or wealthy people to show their status, or rank, in society. Often, the shapes of jewelry symbolized the wearer's importance. King Tut, the boy-king of Egypt, once wore the falcon shown below. The falcon, a **symbol** of the sun-god, appeared many times in Tut's jewelry. Why do you think that a king would wear such symbols? How did the jewelry show Tut's status?

Even though *jewelry* has the word *jewel* in it, it doesn't have to be made of such things as diamonds, emeralds, or rubies. Jewelry can be made of many materials: wood, clay, wire, plastic, beads, and even paper. In this lesson, you will create a shaped pin out of layers of paper.

Egyptian, Falcon Pectoral from the Treasures of Tutankhamen. *Gold pendant inlaid with semiprecious stones and blue glass. The Metropolitan Museum of Art.*

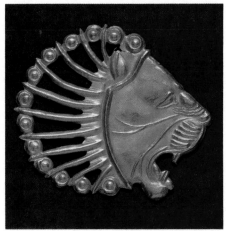

Iran, Bracteate in form of lion head. *550-332 B.C.. Gold. 1⅓"* × *2⅕". The Metropolitan Museum of Art. Gift of Khalil Rabenou, 1956.*

Ireland, Tara pseudopennanular brooch. *8th Century. Bronze gilded with added amber, gold, glass, silver. 8⅕" (length). National Museum of Ireland.*

Creating Art

1. On white paper, draw a simple outline of a shape from nature or a symbol of an event. Cut out your simple shape and trace around it to make seven more shapes exactly like it.

2. Cut out all the shapes. Paste two of them together. Add more and more layers of shapes, until all eight are together in a layer. Apply the paste evenly between layers. You may want to bend the shapes slightly as you paste them in layers.

3. Let the shapes dry overnight. When they are dry, they should be hard. You will be able to use a file on the edges to make them smooth.

4. Paint details on your shaped pin if you like. You might even want to cut out little pieces of colored paper and paste them on top. Coat your shaped object with a gloss. When it is dry, your layered shape will be hard and shiny. Glue a pin to the back of your shape, pin it on, and enjoy!

Art Materials	
White paper	Colored paper
Pencil	Glue
Scissors	Pin
Paste	File or sandpaper
Paints, brush	

Learning Outcomes

1. What are some reasons why people wear jewelry?

2. How did the shape you selected represent either an object from nature or an event important to you?

3. What other kinds of decorative articles besides jewelry do people wear?

95

44 Beads and More Beads

Observing and Thinking

You probably think of beads as just one more example of the many types of jewelry that people wear. Yet, in many primitive cultures throughout history, beads were more than just objects used for decoration. They were used for trading, almost as we use money today. The people of such cultures created beautiful beads out of various materials, from metal and stone to seeds and seashells. Because the beads were so beautiful, and made with such fine craftsmanship, they were as highly valued as gold.

Beads have long been used for important purposes in many cultures. Look at the beaded king's crown from Nigeria. This beaded crown of the Yoruba tribe was believed to honor their god and creator. How many different colors do you see in it? The entire crown was made by hand. Do you think you would have the patience to make a crown such as this?

The American Indians traded in beads. They also used beads to make decorations on many of the things they used. If you look closely at the *martingale,* or horse collar, shown below, you will see how beads were used to create a beautiful flower design.

Yoruba, Nigeria, Royal beaded crown. Late 19th century. Basketry frame with beaded embroidery. 36½" high. The Brooklyn Museum. Carolina A. L. Pratt Fund, Frederick Loser Fund, Carll H. De Silver Fund.

American Indian (Flathead, Montana), Flathead Martingale (horse collar). Late 19th century. Commercial cloth, beads, brass bells. 34" long. Courtesy of the Denver Art Museum, Denver, Colorado.

Liberia, Beaded waist ornament. Peabody Museum—Harvard University. Photograph by Hillel Burger.

Creating Art

1. Use "bead dough" to form beads. Mold the dough into all kinds of shapes. You can make long beads, flat beads, small beads, large beads, round beads, and beads that are like little cubes.

2. While the dough is still soft, poke a hole through each bead using a toothpick. Let the beads dry.

3. You can paint your beads with tempera paint or leave them white. When they are just the way you want them, your teacher will show you how to coat them with a gloss that will keep them from breaking.

4. Arrange the beads in the order you want them to be for your necklace. You may want to experiment with several different orders. Start with the bead you want to have in the center and arrange beads on either side so that the necklace will be **symmetrical**, or the same on both sides. String your necklace and add a fastener.

Art Materials	⬦ THINK SAFETY
"Bead dough"	Water container
Toothpicks	String or thread
Tempera paints	Newspaper
Brush	Necklace fastener

Learning Outcomes

1. What are some of the ways that people in different cultures have used beads?

2. How did you make the design of your necklace symmetrical?

3. In what ways are beads used as both functional objects and decorations?

97

45 Crazy Inventions

Observing and Thinking

Have you ever seen movies about mad scientists who invent strange devices to conquer the world? In real life, inventions are not made by mad scientists, but by talented men and women who have the insight, knowledge, and skill to create products that fill human needs. The inventor is a very special person. He or she must have the artist's imagination and ability to **visualize**, and the scientist's technical knowledge.

One of the greatest inventors of all time was also one of the greatest artists. Leonardo da Vinci, who seemed to be able to do anything well, filled his notebooks with thousands of drawings of inventions he imagined and designed. He designed aircraft, diving suits, submarines, and armored tanks hundreds of years before they became a reality. On the next page you see his design for a helicopter-like device—centuries before anyone had ever heard of such a thing!

Artists sometimes like to play around with ideas for crazy inventions. The *S.S. Pussiewillow II* below is a spaceship that flies with the help of a magic flying carpet, a pedal-operated paddle-wheel, and solar power. Do you think its inventor could have thought of more sensible ways to make it travel in outer space? Paul Klee's *Twittering Machine* is another intriguing invention. For what purpose do you think it was made? Would Leonardo da Vinci have invented it?

Rowland Emett, S.S. Pussiewillow II. © National Air and Space Museum, Smithsonian Institution.

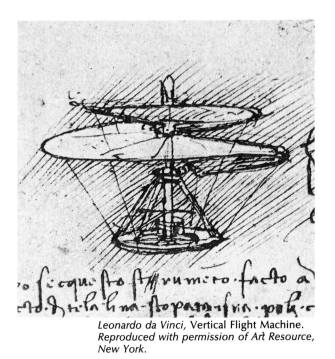

Leonardo da Vinci, Vertical Flight Machine. Reproduced with permission of Art Resource, New York.

Paul Klee, Twittering Machine. 1922. Watercolor, pen and ink. 16¼" × 12". Collection, The Museum of Modern Art, New York. Purchase.

Creating Art

1. Rube Goldberg was an American cartoonist who made fun of America's fascination with gadgets. He would draw imaginary inventions that were designed to accomplish a very simple task, such as swatting a fly, in the most complicated way possible. Think of an invention that you could design. It could be something that doesn't already exist in the world, like a suit that makes people turn invisible. It could be a Rube Goldberg type of device, which does something simple, like opening a jar, in a very complicated, humorous way. Let your imagination run free. Make many sketches of your invention, as Leonardo da Vinci would have done.

2. Make a final drawing of your invention. If your invention works in many steps, you might make a comic strip panel sequence showing the steps the invention goes through to accomplish its purpose. Go over the lines of your drawing with a black felt-tip marker, and color it if you wish. Explain all about your device on the back of your paper or on a separate page.

Art Materials

Imagination	Pencil
A sense of humor	Black felt-tip marker
White drawing paper	Crayons (optional)

Learning Outcomes

1. What qualities do inventors have in common with artists?

2. What steps did you go through to create your crazy invention?

3. Do you think that inventors can get good ideas by letting their imaginations run free? What else do they need?

Exploring Art

The World of the Industrial Designer

What does a car have in common with a tube of toothpaste? Can't guess? Both of them are products of **industrial design**. Industrial design is a field in which products that we use every day are planned and designed for our safe and comfortable use. Industrial designers figure out ways to make products that serve their function well and look attractive. They design everything from toys and televisions to storage containers and detergent bottles. As you can imagine, the industrial designer has to be more than an artist. He or she must understand science, mathematics, and engineering as well.

The examples below are from the Art Center College of Design in Pasadena, California. The students were asked to design cars for major automobile companies. First of all, the students made sketches of car designs. Then, the new designs were made into clay models so that the product could be seen from all sides. If one of these designs were to be accepted by an auto manufacturer, it would eventually be made full-size, in actual materials. Then it would be tested.

Industrial designers do a lot of research of similar products before they begin a design. Your class can become an industrial design school for a while, if you wish. Research the many different varieties of a certain type of product, such as a car, boat, bicycle, or even a wastebasket or piece of furniture. Collect as many magazine pictures as you can, showing these varieties. Then, create your own design for the product, and see if others like it.

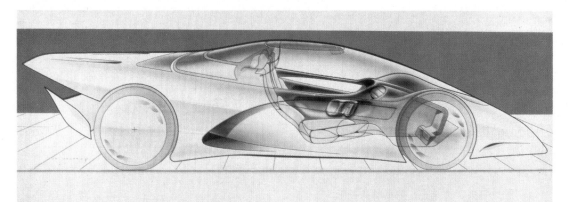

Grant Larson, photographed by Rick Oyama, Corvette Design. Art Center College of Design, Pasadena, California.

GM Lean Machine, Art Center College of Design, Pasadena, California.

Review

Using What You Have Learned

Vasily Kandinsky, a Russian artist, was perhaps the first painter of **abstract** compositions. In the beginning, Kandinsky painted in an open, free style with no shapes or subject matter that the viewer could recognize. Later, he created carefully planned arrangements of geometric shapes. Observe his painting, *Accompanied Contrast*. It was painted with a mixture of oil paint and sand. What can you discover about this painting?

*Vasily Kandinsky, Accompanied Contrast. 1935. Oil with sand on canvas. 38¼″ × 63⅞″.
Solomon R. Guggenheim Museum, New York. Photo: David Heald.*

1. Are there **geometric** and **free-form** shapes in this painting? Give examples of each.

2. Point out some things that Kandinsky did to achieve a sense of depth and distance in this work. How does he make some shapes in the picture seem closer and others farther away?

3. How did Kandinsky achieve **unity**?

4. What kinds of shapes do the **negative spaces** of the painting make? How do these negative spaces help to **balance** the positive shapes?

5. How is color used in this painting? Is it an important part of the **composition**?

6. Would you say that this painting was carefully planned? Why do you say so?

Unit 4

Voyages of Discovery

Robert Vickrey, Gloria's Flowers. *Reproduced with permission of Robert Vickrey.*

Art means making new ideas come alive. Whenever you create art, you discover and express yourself. Throughout this book, you have learned to see with an artist's eyes and discover the richness of the world around you. You have learned that art is a means of communication, and that people of all times and places have used art to express interests and concerns important to all human beings. You have tried different media and techniques, and discovered which of them you most enjoy. But perhaps the most important ingredient in art is something that is difficult to define: the creative **imagination**.

Without imagination, there would be no art, or even the need for art. Your imagination helps you to look at things in new ways and see how they resemble one another. It shows you how to combine very different ideas to make new creations. The imagination takes what is and creates from it what could be—or what could never be! The imagination takes the world of dreams and fantasy seriously. It looks at all the possibilities that exist and asks, "What if?"

With your imagination, you learn to see not just with your eyes but with your mind. Everyone can imagine. Whether you are creating art or simply enjoying the artwork of others, your imagination leads you on a voyage of discovery into what it means to be *you*.

46 Scrimshaw: An American Folk Art

Observing and Thinking

Scrimshaw is the art of carving line drawings into bone or ivory. Carving is an art that is thousands of years old. Scrimshaw, though, is a fairly recent **folk art**. The term *scrimshaw* refers to the whalebone carvings made by the whalers of New England in the 1700s and 1800s. When whaling was an important industry in America, the whalers spent months and even years at sea. To pass the time, they would draw beautiful, intricate designs on the polished bones and teeth of the captured whales. Often, their scrimshaw drawings told of their adventures at sea.

A piece of sharkskin glued to a block of wood made fine sandpaper. The scrimshaw artist would sand the whale tooth or bone to a smooth surface, then **engrave**, or finely cut, a picture into it using sharp tools. To bring out the finished design, the engraver would fill the lines with colored inks.

Today, whales are protected by law, so scrimshaw artists use hardened ivory nuts from the ivory palm of South America instead. You do not need whalebone or ivory nuts to practice the art of scrimshaw, however: plaster of paris will do.

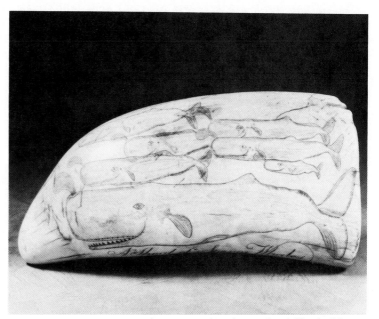

Anonymous American artist, A Shoal of Sperm Whales. *December 1818. 7⅛″. Mystic Seaport Collection, Connecticut.*

4. When your drawing is complete, blow off any specks of plaster that remain. Darken the engraved lines with a fine-line black felt-tip marker, and display your scrimshaw piece.

Art Materials	
Plaster of paris	Pencil
Waxed paper	Drawing paper
Water, paper towels	Engraving tools
Water container	Black felt-tip marker

Creating Art

1. Mix plaster of paris and drop spoonfuls of it onto waxed paper. While it is still wet, form it into the shape you want to carve into. Perhaps you would like to make a shape like a whale's tooth. Let the plaster shape dry for a day or two.

2. Draw the shape of your plaster piece on paper and plan a drawing or design for your scrimshaw.

3. Choose one of your drawings and draw it on the plaster with a sharp pencil. Then use a sharp nail, file, or other metal object to engrave the lines of your drawing. Scrimshaw has very fine lines and details. Make your lines as thin as you can.

Learning Outcomes

1. What is scrimshaw? Why did whalers make scrimshaw pieces?

2. Describe the design you chose to carve in your scrimshaw piece.

3. What other examples of American folk art can you think of? Can you explain why a folk art is different from many kinds of art you would see in a museum?

47 *Stars and Stripes Forever*

Observing and Thinking

Have you ever thought of the American flag as an example of excellent design? Look at the flag in your classroom as though it were a painting. Describe it in art terms. Does it use lines, shapes, and colors to form **patterns**? Is there **rhythm** in the patterns? In what ways is the flag a well-designed work of art?

The American flag is one example of the many visual **symbols** around us. Most of the symbols that we see daily, such as traffic signs, consist of simple shapes and limited colors. For thousands of years, the symbols used in flags have remained much the same. Flags often include simple geometric shapes and **stylized**, or simplified, figures of such objects as stars, birds, the sun, half-moons, and crosses. The seven basic flag colors—red, white, blue, black, green, orange, and yellow—have also remained unchanged for hundreds of years.

Artists have often used the American flag as an image in works of art. Study *Three Flags* by Jasper Johns. If you look closely, you will see that his flag contains only forty-eight stars in a regular **repeating** pattern. The flag in your classroom has fifty stars in an **alternating** pattern. Do you know why Johns' flag is different? (For a clue, look at the date the painting was made.) What other repeating or alternating patterns do you see in the flag? Do these patterns give the flag a sense of rhythm and movement?

Jasper Johns, Three Flags. *1958. Encaustic on canvas. 30⅞″ × 45½″ × 5″. Collection of Whitney Museum of American Art. 50th Anniversary gift of the Gilman Foundation, Inc., the Lauder Foundation, A. Alfred Taubman, an anonymous donor (and purchase). Acq. #80.32*

Dodge MacKnight, Flags, Milk Street, Boston. *Watercolor. 23¾″ × 16¹³⁄₁₆″. Museum of Fine Arts, Boston. Bequest of Mrs. Stephen S. FitzGerald. 65.2114*

Creating Art

1. Think about all the things that America means to you. Pretend that you have been asked to create a new flag that symbolizes everything your country stands for. What colors and shapes will you use? Try to limit your colors and shapes so that you can create a simple but striking and unified design. You may use red, white, and blue if you wish, but you should use them in shapes and patterns that are different from the Star-Spangled Banner.

2. Sketch a design for your flag. When you have made a design that you like, draw it on a piece of paper. You may use colored paper for the background, if you wish. Choose colors that you feel are symbols of different qualities.

3. You will make your flag out of pieces of colored construction paper. Just as a flagmaker would cut out and sew pieces of material together, cut out and paste pieces of colored paper together to make your flag. Think about the patterns you are creating. How can you create unity in your flag design?

Art Materials	THINK SAFETY
Drawing paper	Pencil
Colored construction paper	Scissors
	Paste

Learning Outcomes

1. How are lines, shapes, and colors used in the American flag to create pattern and a sense of rhythm?

2. What qualities did you try to show in your flag? How did you show them?

3. Compare the two paintings shown in this lesson. How is the flag used as the center of interest in each?

48 *The Sun: A Symbol in Art*

Observing and Thinking

If you looked through a book on the history of art in all cultures, you would see that **symbols** of the sun have been used in every art form, from painting and sculpture to clothing and jewelry. Look at this feather *tunic,* or jacket, from Peru. It is from the time of the Incas. The Incas worshipped the sun, and used many pictures of it in their art. Do you see how the sun is shown in the center of the tunic? It is perfectly balanced and **symmetrical**. If you divided it down the middle, you would see that the design is the same on both sides. How does symmetrical balance make this a good design? Think about the purpose of the tunic. Can you think of a practical reason why the artist would have placed the sun directly in the middle of the jacket?

Do you know what the Smithsonian Institution is? In the Smithsonian Mace shown on page 109, the sun stands for knowledge and wisdom. Why would the sun be a good symbol for these values? Do you see how the lion holds the sun off to one side? Although the mace figure is balanced, it is not the same on both sides. The sun is off to one side in **asymmetrical** balance. How does this kind of balance help move your eyes directly to the symbol of the sun?

Peru, Inca, 1100-1400, Feather Tunic. Rows of feathers knotted on cords and stitched to plain weave cotton ground. 71" × 33". Los Angeles County Museum of Art. Gift of Mr. and Mrs. William T. Senson, Jr.

The Smithsonian Mace. *Smithsonian Institution, Washington, D.C.*

Creating Art

1. Think about all the possible ways you could use the sun as a symbol. Perhaps it means something special to you that no one else has thought of. Be as original as you can, as though you are the first person who has ever tried to draw and paint the sun.

2. Make one or more sketches of the sun. Choose your favorite sketch and make a large drawing. You may wish to use math tools, such as a ruler and compass. Decide where to place the sun symbol in your painting. Will it be directly in the middle of your paper in symmetrical balance, or will you place it off to one side in asymmetrical balance?

3. What colors will you use in your painting? Mix the colors you will use. Think about using cool colors and shades for **contrast** in your painting. You may wish to use unexpected colors for your sun.

4. When your painting is complete, display it with others from your class. Did everyone make a different kind of sun? How many different kinds of suns are there?

Art Materials	
White drawing paper	Mixing tray
Pencil	Water container
Tempera paints	Newspapers
Brush	Compass, ruler (optional)
Paper towels	

Learning Outcomes

1. What are some ways that artists have used the sun in art? Can you name some things the sun has been used to symbolize?

2. How did you create your sun symbol design? What kind of balance did you use? Why?

3. If you could create a sun symbol in any medium, which medium would you use? Why do you say so?

109

49 Pictures Tell About the Past

Observing and Thinking

Artists have many purposes in making works of art. They may be expressing an idea or feeling important to them. They may want to point out something that is wrong with the society in which they live. They may simply want to create something beautiful. Many times, whether they intend to or not, artists act as historians. They paint **realistic** scenes, showing what life was like in their time.

Winslow Homer painted many scenes of country life. In this 1871 painting, he shows what a one-room schoolhouse in the country was like. What details do you notice in this picture? Can you make some judgments about what school must have been like in the days when this picture was painted?

Charles Burchfield painted many realistic pictures of life in American small towns. Do you think that he caught the mood and feeling of this little town that he knew? What would life in this town be like?

Frederic Remington studied and painted cowboys and Indians, making a visual record that shows us what life was like in the Old West. In *The Fall of the Cowboy*, Remington shows how the free-roaming life of the cowboy was being changed by the introduction of barbed wire fences to keep cattle from wandering. He thought that the fences would lead to the end of the cowboy's way of life. How does this painting show what Remington felt about this turn of events?

Winslow Homer, The Country School. 1871. Oil on canvas. 21⅜″ × 38⅜″. The Saint Louis Art Museum, Museum Purchase. 123:1946

Charles Burchfield, Old Tavern at Hammondsville, Ohio. *Addison Gallery of American Art, Phillips Academy, Andover, Massachusetts.*

Frederic Remington, The Fall of the Cowboy. *1895. Oil on canvas. 25" × 35⅛". Courtesy Amon Carter Museum, Fort Worth.*

Creating Art

1. Think of a subject to paint that would let future generations know a little bit about what your life is like. You may want to paint a picture of your classroom, showing as many details as you can. You could paint a favorite part of your town, or show a part of your community that is changing rapidly. Carefully observe the place you want to paint. Make sketches that you can refer to for your final painting. Find what is most important in your subject.

2. Choose your best sketch and make it into a finished drawing. Then paint it, using realistic colors. Pretend that your painting will go into a time capsule that will be opened a thousand years from now. When the people of that time look at your painting, what will they be able to tell about life in our time?

Art Materials

White drawing paper	Mixing tray
Pencil	Water, paper towels
Tempera paints	Water container
Brush	Newspaper

Learning Outcomes

1. What are some reasons why an artist may create a work of art?

2. What did you show in your painting that would give future generations an idea of what your life is like today?

3. Compare the moods of each of the paintings in this lesson. In what ways did the artists make their pictures more personal than photographs could be?

111

50 Telling Stories with Totem Poles

Observing and Thinking

Have you ever seen a **totem pole**? The Northwest Indians of the United States and Canada carved images of their tribal history, traditions, and legends into long poles of wood before they ever developed a written language. The images they carved, called **totems**, were of special people, animals, fish, and birds that were important to the history of each tribe. The totem poles recorded important events and told stories without words.

Totem poles were created from tall trees that had been split in half and hollowed out.

The totem images were carved into the wood and painted with earth colors, such as reds and browns. Although the totem faces were simple, exaggerated shapes, they represented real things.

The Canadian artist Emily Carr made a special study of the totem poles of the Northwest Indians. For years, she dedicated herself to recording these powerful images in her paintings, honoring the history and traditions of the Indians whose lives were quickly being changed by the presence of Europeans.

Emily Carr, Queen Charlotte Islands Totem. *76.2 cm × 53.8 cm. Vancouver Art Gallery, British Columbia.*

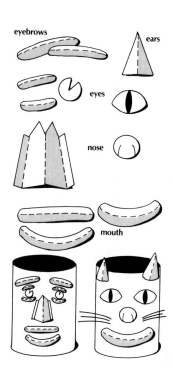

Creating Art

1. Think back over the school year. Try to remember something special that has happened to you. How could you represent that event with a totem image? Make some sketches of a totem face you could create. You may look through books on totem poles for ideas, but your images should be your very own invention.

2. Fold and glue tagboard or thick paper to form a cylinder. You may use a half-gallon ice cream container if you wish, and cover it with paper.

3. You can make **three-dimensional** features for your paper totem face by cutting and folding your paper, then gluing, stapling, or taping the edges together. Remember that totem faces, like human faces, are **symmetrical**. Each side will be identical to the other. You can paint extra features on your totem image when you are through making the face.

4. When you are satisfied with your totem face, explain the story that it represents.

Art Materials		THINK SAFETY
Tagboard or thick paper	Drawing paper	
Scissors	Glue	
Tempera paints and brush	Tape	
Pencil	Stapler	

Learning Outcomes

1. Why did the Northwest Indians carve totem poles? What do the images mean?

2. How did you decide on a type of totem face to create? How did you make your face look like a real totem?

3. What qualities of totem poles did artist Emily Carr express in her painting?

51 Found Object Masks

Observing and Thinking

Have you ever worn a mask? How did it make you feel? Did other people react to you in a different way? What are some reasons or occasions you would wear a mask?

Masks are very important objects in primitive cultures. Many primitive peoples believe that spirit powers dwell in all natural things. When they make masks, they honor the spirit powers in the natural objects they use to create the mask. Every mask they make contains its own spirit. Because of this, the making of masks is considered a sacred duty that is carried out by special mask-makers.

Masks used in primitive cultures are made of materials found in the everyday environment. Wood or turtle shells are among the materials used for main parts of masks. Some masks are woven from corn husks, straw, or *raffia,* a type of palm. The mask-maker creates **variety** and interest by putting unique details on the mask with feathers, shells, bark, seeds, fibers, and other natural objects. These details form **textures** and interesting **patterns** of lines, shapes, and colors on the masks.

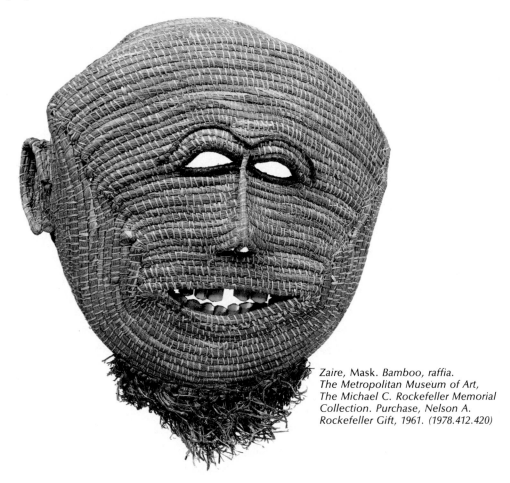

Zaire, Mask. Bamboo, raffia.
The Metropolitan Museum of Art,
The Michael C. Rockefeller Memorial
Collection. Purchase, Nelson A.
Rockefeller Gift, 1961. (1978.412.420)

Iroquois cornhusk mask. *Reproduction courtesy of United States Department of the Interior, Indian Arts and Crafts Board.*

Creating Art

1. Make a collection of natural materials that you find outdoors, such as leaves, bark, pinecones, acorns, and feathers. If you wish, you may also bring dried beans, string, and similar materials from home.

2. Pretend that you and your classmates are all part of a primitive tribe. Discuss what kind of tribe you are. For what purpose will your tribe use masks? What kind of mask will you make for your tribe?

3. Cut an oval larger than your head from a piece of cardboard. Use an object such as blunt scissors to **score** your cardboard mask down the middle. This means that you will make a groove that will help you to bend the two halves of your mask easily. Poke or cut holes for eyes.

4. Glue your found objects onto your mask. Form interesting patterns of lines, shapes, colors, and textures. Perhaps the decorations you make will have a special symbolic meaning for your tribe.

5. Add string, yarn, or other materials to make hair. Wear your mask. Your class may want to invent a ceremony for your tribe to perform.

Art Materials	THINK SAFETY
Cardboard	Found objects
Scissors	Objects from home
Glue	Pencil

Learning Outcomes

1. What are some of the reasons why a person or a culture would use a mask?

2. How did you add pattern to your mask? Can you explain how the decorations you made express your tribe?

3. How are masks like faces? How are they different? If you made a mask of your face, what would it look like?

52 Puppets for the Fun of It

Observing and Thinking

A puppet is a movable figure controlled by a person. Puppets have amused and taught people for thousands of years. Just about every culture and civilization seems to have had puppets of one kind or another. Even today, modern audiences love to watch the colorful antics of puppets. Perhaps you are a fan of such famous movie heroes as E.T. and Yoda. Both characters are really just advanced types of puppets.

There are several main types of puppets. **Marionettes**, or string puppets, are controlled from above by strings or wires. Some large and complicated marionettes have to be operated by more than one person at a time. Marionettes are capable of more kinds of movements than other puppets. They have even been used to act out operas! The wom-

an shown below is a professional **puppeteer**, making her own marionette for a puppet show. The Leprechaun is just one of many marionettes she has created.

Rod puppets and **shadow puppets**, two other major puppet types, are controlled from below by sticks and rods. The most commonly used puppet, though, is the **hand puppet**. A hand puppet can be made of many kinds of materials, from paper sacks to socks. Even though hand puppets are a very simple form of puppet, some of the most famous puppets have been of this type. The Muppet characters Kermit and Miss Piggy are special versions of the hand puppet.

In this lesson, you will invent and create a hand puppet from your own collection of—believe it or not—junk!

Courtesy of Puppets Please

Courtesy of Puppets Please

Creating Art

1. Students created the puppets shown above from "throwaways"—egg cartons, paper plates, cardboard tubes, old clothes, and other "junk" materials. Make your own collection of natural and man-made found objects that you think you could use to create your own puppet.

2. What will your puppet be? A person? An animal? A monster? Only you can decide—so use your imagination in combining your odds and ends of throwaways. Use glue, staples, string, tape, or anything else you need to fasten things together. Add details such as eyes, hair, and feathers to your puppet. Use paint, crayons, or felt-tip markers for finishing touches. Remember that your puppet is **three-dimensional**; complete it all the way around so that it looks good from every side. Practice using your puppet.

3. Puppets are not made to sit on a shelf, but to act in puppet plays. Get together with a classmate and make up a story to act out, or look through books for stories you can adapt for a puppet play.

Art Materials	
Throwaway items	Colored markers, crayons, or paints
Masking tape, white glue, and other fasteners (as needed)	Scissors

Learning Outcomes

1. What are some of the main types of puppets used all over the world?

2. What materials did you use to create your puppet character? How did you decide on the type of character to create?

3. What can a puppet do that a person cannot do? How can you make a puppet "come to life"?

117

53 *Out of the Ordinary*

Observing and Thinking

People often ask artists where they get their ideas. The answer is: Everywhere. Artists can find ideas for artwork in even the most ordinary things. What could be more ordinary than a chair? Yet, as you can see from the pictures on these pages, even a chair can inspire an artist to be creative. All it takes is an open mind, a willingness to experiment, and—yes—a sense of humor.

Joanne Syrop's colorful *Throne 1* below is based on the idea of a rocking chair. But what a rocking chair this is! Do you notice that the "head" seems to be going in the opposite direction from the many pairs of feet? What is the effect of this?

Lucas Samaras' *Chair Transformation Number 16,* below, is not like any chair you would see in a living room. How do you think he got the idea for this chair?

Artists often get creative ideas from the different materials they use. The chairs on the next page are made of unusual materials. The nature of the materials helped to decide the final form the chairs would take. Could you sit on these chairs? What do you think they would feel like?

In this lesson, you will think of ways to transform an ordinary object, making it something "out of the ordinary."

Joanne Syrop, Throne I. *Painted wood construction. About 24" × 20". Courtesy of the artist.*

Lucas Samaras, Chair Transformation No. 16. *1969-1970. Synthetic polymer on wood. 30" × 15" × 28". Collection of Whitney Museum of American Art, New York.*

Gunnar Aagaard Andersen, Armchair, 1964, polyurethane, 29½" × 44¼" × 35¼". Collection, The Museum of Modern Art, New York. Gift of the designer.

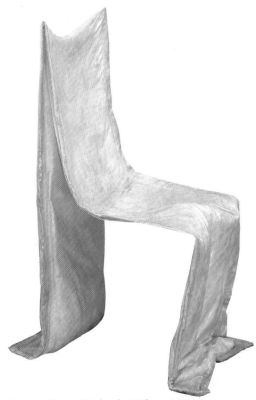

Gaetano Pesce, "Golgotha" Chair, 1974, molded fiberglass cloth and resin, 39" × 25" × 16¼". Collection, The Museum of Modern Art, New York. Estee and Joseph Lauder Design Fund.

Creating Art

1. Collect and study photographs of a common household object that you would like to transform. You may wish to be creative with a sofa, refrigerator, vacuum cleaner, bathtub, bed, or some other object that is as common and ordinary as a chair.

2. Fold a piece of paper into four sections. In each section of your paper, draw a different **variation** of the object you have chosen to transform. Use your imagination and think of all the ways you could transform the object. You could change its shape. You could add extra parts to it. You could show it made out of an unexpected material, such as a bathtub made out of fur. You can use strange colors and designs. Draw four variations of your "ordinary" household object, making each one very different from the rest. Share the fun of your "out of the ordinary" designs with the rest of the class.

Art Materials	
White drawing paper	Magazine photos
Pencil	Crayons or colored pencils

Learning Outcomes

1. Name some ways that artists can get ideas for their work.

2. How many ways did you transform your common object? How did you think of your ideas?

3. Which of the chairs pictured in the lesson shows the most imagination? Which shows the best sense of humor?

54 All Kinds of Comics

Observing and Thinking

What part of the newspaper do you enjoy the most? If you are like a lot of people, you probably look forward to reading the comic section. Comics provide entertainment for millions of people of all ages.

Perhaps the most popular form of comic is the **comic strip**. Most comic strips consist of several boxes, called **panels**, showing a sequence of action. Comic strips usually feature a continuing cast of characters. People like to follow the adventures of the characters they have come to know.

Some newspaper comics are only one panel long. This type of comic often does not have continuing characters. Instead, the artist, or **cartoonist**, shows a single funny idea or action. This kind of strip can be challenging to create. Why?

Comic books were introduced in the 1910s. The first comic books were reprints of strips that had originally appeared in newspapers. Later, comic books started to feature all-new material. In comic books, many panels are used to show the action.

Study these examples of newspaper comic strips. What would you say are some of the unique qualities of comic art?

Gary Larson, *The Far Side*. Copyright 1985 Universal Press Syndicate. Reprinted with permission. All rights reserved.

Jim Davis, Garfield™ *comic strip.* © 1980 United Feature Syndicate, Inc.

120

Creating Art

1. Cartoonists usually **simplify** their characters, focusing on a few main features. Study how cartoonists have simplified the characters in these examples. Experiment by making some cartoon-like characters from your imagination. It's important not to copy the characters created by another cartoonist. Comic characters are copyrighted. No one has the right to draw them except the creator.

2. Think of a funny idea or incident you could show in one panel, or a sequence you could show in several panels. Plan out your comic with sketches first. Make your pictures simple. Will you use speech balloons for each character, or write the words underneath each panel?

3. Draw your comic strip or one-panel cartoon. Go over the lines of your drawing with a black felt marker. If you color your comic art with colored felt markers, use bold, basic colors such as those you would find in the Sunday paper comics.

Art Materials	
Pencil and eraser	Black marker
White drawing paper	Colored markers
Ruler	

Learning Outcomes

1. What are some of the forms that comic art can take?

2. What kind of comic did you draw? How did you plan a sequence of action?

3. What is your favorite comic character or comic strip? Why?

55 *A Book to Flip Over*

Observing and Thinking

Do you like to watch animated films? **Animation** is the art of putting a sequence of drawings together to produce the illusion of motion. A reel of animated film is made up of thousands of pictures. Each picture, or **frame**, shows a very gradual change in motion. Look at the scene from Walt Disney's *Fantasia* on page 123. It is only one frame from a complex sequence of action. Full-length cartoons can consist of as many as a million drawings. A team of professional **animators** may take years to complete a film.

Animation only became possible once people started to understand how human and animal figures move. In the 1860s, people began to experiment with photography.

Eadweard Muybridge, one of these early experimenters, decided to study how horses move. He set up twenty-four cameras to take pictures of a horse and rider in motion. Later, he projected the pictures one after another in sequence. He found that this created the illusion of motion. His experiments led to the invention of the motion picture.

Today, animators use photography and movies to help them understand how they can make their characters move realistically. They make animation sketches to plan out sequences of action.

In this lesson, you will make a **flip book**, a kind of short animated "movie" on paper.

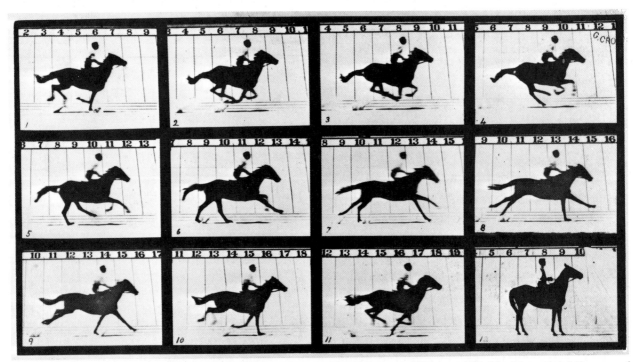

Eadweard Muybridge, Motion Studies of Horse and Rider. c. 1870. The International Museum of Photography at George Eastman House.

© 1940 Walt Disney Productions

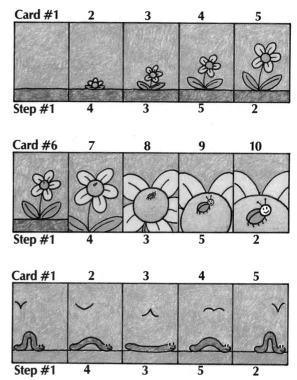

Creating Art

1. Think of a simple action you would like to show in your flip book. Place five blank index cards side by side. On the first card, draw the picture that will begin your action sequence. On the fifth card, draw the action that will end the sequence. This is how animators work.

2. Now, draw the action on cards number 2 through 4. This will be the action that happens in the middle. These cards are called **in-betweens**. Show a noticeable change from card to card, as in the examples shown above.

3. To see your drawings in motion, stack the cards in order. Number 5 should be on top, and number 1 on the bottom. Grip the top edge of your flip book with one hand, and with your thumb flip the pages from back to front. Gently arch the cards. Let your thumb release them one by one.

4. You can add more drawings to the "in-between" part of your flip book. When you have completed the action sequence, staple or tape the pages together at the top.

Art Materials

Blank index cards	Crayons or colored pencils
Pencil	
	Staple or tape

Learning Outcomes

1. How did the experiments of Eadweard Muybridge lead to a greater understanding of motion?

2. How did you create a sequence of motion in your flip book?

3. Why is it important for an animator to understand how motion occurs? How can animators study motion?

56 Designing a Book Jacket

Observing and Thinking

Have you ever heard the saying, "You can't judge a book by its cover"? How many times have you read a book because you liked the cover? Did the cover give you a good idea of what the book would be like?

Many hardcover books are covered by paper sleeves, or **jackets**. Study the jacket of one of your favorite books. Notice how it is designed. The front cover will often show a picture done by the **illustrator** of the book. The back cover may show an illustration, a photograph of the author, or even information about the book. Open up the book, and you may find further information on the jacket flaps. There may be information about the story, author, or artist that makes you want to read the book.

The illustrator of a book usually does not design the jacket. Instead, a specially trained **graphic artist**, called a designer, is chosen for this task. The designer may use one of the illustrator's pictures, but the lettering and design, or **layout**, of the jacket are equally important. The jacket designer must think like an advertiser as well as an artist. He or she must find ways to make the jacket appealing as well as informative. A well-designed jacket will attract attention among the hundreds of books on library or bookstore shelves.

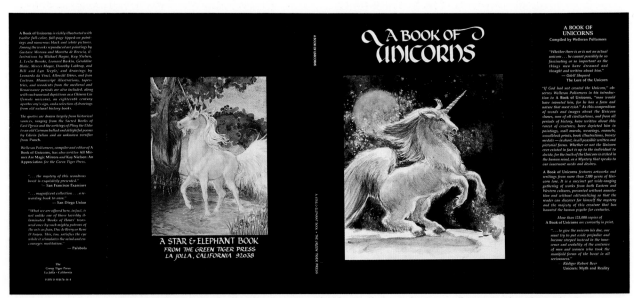

Cover art from A Book of Unicorns, compiled by Welleran Poltarnees. Illustration by Alexandra Day.
Copyright © 1978 by The Green Tiger Press. Reproduced by permission of the publisher. All rights reserved.

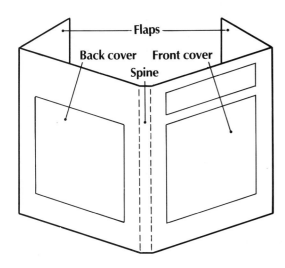

Creating Art

1. Study several jackets from books that you like. Get some ideas for a jacket that you will design for a book you know or a book you would like to write. Using a ruler, measure a hardcover book carefully. Measure the height from top to bottom. Measure the length from the back cover to the front cover. In this measurement, include the width of the spine, or the "backbone" of the book, where the pages are sewn or glued together.

2. Use a large piece of paper to make your jacket. Measure the paper to fit the book you measured. Allow several inches of overlap on each end of your paper so that you can fold the jacket around to make inside flaps.

3. Draw the front and back covers for your book. The illustration you draw should tell about an important part of the story or show the main characters. Include lettering for the title and the author's name.

Write the author and title on the spine neatly. Write some information on the inside jacket flaps. Put your jacket around the book for which it was measured, and display it with others from your class.

Art Materials		THINK SAFETY
Book	Large piece of white paper	
Ruler and scissors		
Pencil	Crayons	

Learning Outcomes

1. Why are book jackets so carefully designed? Why are they important in attracting the reader's attention?

2. What decisions did you make in creating your jacket design? What part of your jacket do you think is most successful?

3. What do you think is the most important part of a jacket design?

57 Who Am I?

Observing and Thinking

If you could paint a picture showing yourself as you are right now, what would it look like? Many artists make pictures of themselves to show how they change over the years. These **self-portraits** are more interesting than photographs would be because they reveal what the artists think about themselves.

Vincent van Gogh painted more than twenty self-portraits. He had started to paint late in life and was an intense, driven man. This portrait was painted during one of the most peaceful times of his life. Yet, he killed himself three years later. Do you see some evidence of how troubled he was in the self-portrait shown below?

Vincent van Gogh, Self-Portrait. 1887. Oil on canvas. 13¾″ × 10½″. The Detroit Institute of Arts. City of Detroit Purchase.

Dutch artist Judith Leyster was one of the few women painters of the **Renaissance**. What can you tell about her character by looking at this picture? Do you think she was a happy person? What does the picture she is painting tell about her as a person?

Judith Leyster, Self-Portrait. c. 1635. Canvas. 29⅜″ × 25⅜″. National Gallery of Art, Washington, D.C. Gift of Mr. and Mrs. Robert Woods Bliss.

Edward Hopper and Mary Cassatt were two famous American painters. Hopper painted pictures that often seem lonely and empty of people. He drew the self-portrait on page 127 when he was about twenty-one. What can you tell about him from this drawing? Cassatt painted many pictures of mothers and children. What kind of a person do you think she was? Does the portrait show this?

Edward Hopper (1882–1967), Self-Portrait. 1903. Charcoal on paper. 16½" × 12". National Portrait Gallery, Smithsonian Institution, Washington, D.C.

Mary Cassatt, Self-Portrait. 1880. Watercolor on paper. 13" × 9⅝". National Portrait Gallery, Smithsonian Institution, Washington, D.C.

Creating Art

1. Using a mirror, look carefully at your face. Although everyone has the same features—eyes, nose, mouth—each part is shaped differently for each person. Look at your face and its features before you start to draw.

2. Lightly sketch the shape of your head. Make small marks to show where your eyes, nose, mouth, and ears would be.

3. Use your pencil to draw the details of your face. Look in the mirror many times as you draw. Draw the shapes that you see.

4. Place your self-portrait where you can see it at a distance. Look in the mirror and at your picture. Do you need to add any details to your drawing?

5. Paint over your finished portrait with a watercolor wash. Use colors that express a mood. You may want to run several colors together. Display your self-portrait.

Art Materials

White paper	Water, paper towels
Pencil	
Mirror	Mixing tray
Watercolor paints	Water container
Brush	Newspaper

Learning Outcomes

1. What is a self-portrait? What are some reasons why artists create them?

2. What did you show about yourself in your self-portrait?

3. How does each art example in the lesson show the subject's personality?

58 You're Invited to a Dinner Party

Observing and Thinking

Judy Chicago is an American artist who is concerned about women's rights. She speaks out in support of women through her artwork. Her best-known work is *The Dinner Party.* It is a huge table shaped like a triangle. Each side has thirteen place settings honoring famous women from history, science, and the arts. The plates, knives, forks, cups, and place mats are all handmade **symbols** of the women they represent. The names of these women are written on the ceramic floor. Four hundred women worked with Judy Chicago for five years to create this work.

Study the plate design for the woman named Sacajawea (sak-uh-juh-wee′-uh). She was an American Indian translator in the famous Lewis and Clark Expedition. Does the **geometric** design of this plate remind you of Indian designs you have seen? Does it look a bit like a butterfly?

Caroline Herschel was an astronomer of the late eighteenth and early nineteenth centuries. Although she spent her life helping her more famous brother, William Herschel, she made many discoveries on her own. She was determined to be independent, and taught herself the complicated mathematics that she needed in her research. She was the first woman to discover a comet. In her lifetime, Caroline Herschel never received the fame she had earned. Judy Chicago symbolized her with a single eye in the center of wings. Why is this a good symbol for a woman who studied the stars?

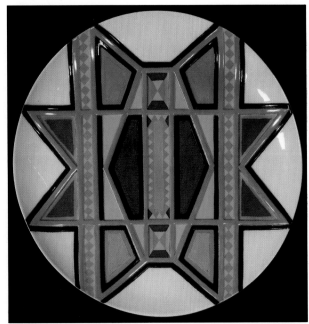

Judy Chicago, Sacajawea plate *from* The Dinner Party. *14 inches in diameter. © 1979 Judy Chicago. Photograph by Don Miller.*

Judy Chicago, Caroline Herschel plate *from* The Dinner Party. *14 inches in diameter. © 1979 Judy Chicago. Photograph by Don Miller.*

Judy Chicago, The Dinner Party. *47 feet on each side.*
© 1979 Judy Chicago. Photograph by Michael Alexander.

Judy Chicago, Kathleen Schneider, and Susan Hill with Fertile Goddess runner. © 1979 Judy Chicago. Photographer unknown.

Creating Art

1. Think of a famous person, man or woman, for whom you would like to design a place setting. What colors and symbols could you use to represent this person? Use a circular piece of paper the size of a real plate to draw your design. Your design should show **radial balance**, with parts coming out from a center, like spokes on a wheel. You can achieve such balance in a circular shape by dividing the plate into equal sections, like slices of pie. You can also place a design in the center or around the edges of the circle. Experiment and see what works best.

2. Make a place mat out of a large piece of paper. Repeat the symbols you used in the plate. Draw and cut out the rest of the place setting: knives, forks, spoons, a napkin, and a drinking cup. These can be any shape you like. You may leave them solid or make designs on them.

3. Choose the colors you will use. With crayons or oil pastels, color in your designs. Think about putting your colors together in attractive ways. Will you use all warm or all cool colors, a **monochrome** color scheme, or **complementary** colors? What do the colors you chose symbolize?

4. Get together with the rest of the class and set a table for your own "dinner party" of famous people.

Art Materials ◆ THINK SAFETY

Circular paper	White drawing paper
Scissors	Crayons or oil pastels
Pencil	

Learning Outcomes

1. How did Judy Chicago represent famous women in *The Dinner Party*?

2. What color and design symbols did you use to represent your famous person? Why did you choose them?

3. Can artists have an effect on public opinion? What might *The Dinner Party* make people think about?

59 *Strange Creations*

Observing and Thinking

Did you ever play with toys that had removable pieces you could switch around to make new toys? When you did this kind of recombining of parts, you were doing something that many artists do. Artists use their imaginations to see how different things can be put together to form new creations.

Mario Mariotti, Choir, from the book Humands. *Photo reproduced by permission of Green Tiger Press, La Jolla, California. Copyright 1982 by La Nuova Italia Editrice, Florence, Italy. All rights reserved.*

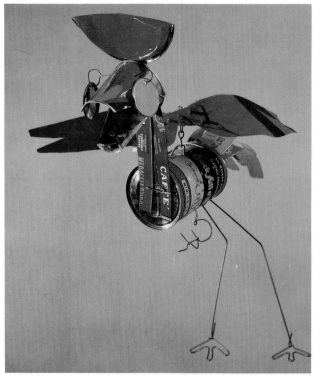

Alexander Calder, Chock. 1972. Metal. 11" × 28" × 22". Collection of Whitney Museum of American Art. Gift of the artist.

Alexander Calder is a famous American artist who often works with wire and metal. His *Chock*, shown above, is a fantasy bird figure made out of a coffee can and other pieces of scrap metal. This kind of art is called **assemblage**. It shows how artists can look at materials and see ways of putting them together to make something new.

Mario Mariotti, an Italian artist, loves to see how different things can resemble each other. He discovered that he could paint and pose his hands to make many clever human and animal figures. Because he knows how to see like an artist, he can look at many things and see the connections between them, or the ways that they are similar.

The shape of a toy car reminded Pablo Picasso of a baboon's head. Do you think he discovered this resemblance by accident? Do certain car shapes remind you of other things, such as particular animals?

In this lesson, you will think of ways that two or more very different things can be put together to form a unique creation.

Pablo Picasso, Baboon and Young. 1951. Bronze (cast 1955), after found objects. 21" high, base 13¼" × 6⅞". Collection, The Museum of Modern Art, New York. Mrs. Simon Guggenheim Fund.

Patrick Woodroffe, Mickey and Friend. 1976. Reproduced with permission from Simon and Schuster.

Creating Art

1. Take some time to look for resemblances between things. You do this all the time when you look at clouds and see shapes in them. Bring some objects from home, such as old toys, that might give you ideas for creative combinations.

2. When you have an idea for the strange combination you could create, make an "instruction sheet" for it. Pretend that you are drawing visual directions for putting something together, like a stereo or bicycle. In this case, though, you will be drawing instructions for putting together a fantastic creation that no one has ever seen before. Use your imagination. Draw all the parts that would be used in your combination of objects. Show how they could be put together to make something new and unique. When you are finished, ask yourself this question: If you gave the instructions to a friend, along with the necessary materials, could he or she make the strange creation?

Art Materials	
Drawing paper	Objects from home
Pencil	
Crayons or colored pencils	Your imagination

Learning Outcomes

1. Name some ways that artists can combine things to make new creations.

2. What materials would you use to make your strange combination? Did you create easy-to-follow directions?

3. Which of the artworks shown in the lesson do you think is most creative? Why?

131

60 Building a World

Observing and Thinking

Do you like to read science fiction books, or watch science fiction movies? Do you know the difference between science fiction and fantasy? Good science fiction is based on a solid knowledge of science. Science fiction creators ask themselves the question, "What if?" What if a planet had no land masses and was covered by one big ocean? What if that planet had two small suns and no moon? The writer would use proven scientific principles to invent life-forms and an ecology that would likely exist on such a planet.

Once a year, on the West Coast, scientists, artists, and writers join forces in a conference called *Contact*. These creative people share ideas about our future in space, and the possibility of life on other planets. They work together to develop a possible world. They first determine what kind of sun it will have, how large the world will be, and what kind of land features it will have. Once they know

these things, they invent the life-forms that might evolve on such a planet. The artists draw and paint pictures of the alien world and its life-forms. Then they build **three-dimensional** models, in such **media** as ceramics, of the creatures they invented. When the "world-building" conference is over, the scientists, artists, and writers have created a world that doesn't exist, but could.

In this lesson, you and your classmates will collaborate, or join together, on the creation of your own "possible world."

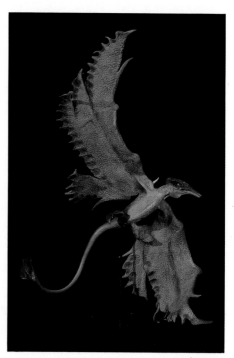

© Joel Hagen

© Joel Hagen

© Joel Hagen

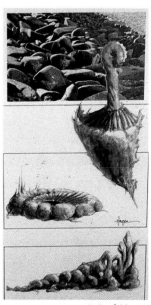
© Joel Hagen

Creating Art

1. As a class, discuss the kind of world you want to create. Make a decision about how large the world will be, how many suns or moons it will have, what kind of land masses it will have, and so on. Consult encyclopedias, as well as science books. Try to make your world believable and based on scientific fact. If you want to, make a classroom model of your world, using an old globe or a papier-mâché sphere.

2. What kind of life-forms would live on your world? Draw pictures of your alien landscape and the creatures that live there. Will any of the creatures be intelligent? Will they look like us? What will their culture be like?

3. Your class can create a **diorama** of the alien world. Choose some people to paint the landscape background, some to make three-dimensional models of creatures, and others to put in details using found objects such as rocks, sticks, sand, and the like. What did you learn from your world-building experience?

Art Materials

Drawing paper	Assorted materials for world-building,
Pencils	such as a globe, paints, papier-mâché, glue, found
Reference materials	objects, etc.

Learning Outcomes

1. How can the fields of art and science join together to create new ideas?

2. Tell about your alien world. How did you use your knowledge of both science and art to create a believable world?

3. What is the value of a conference like *Contact*? Can you think of other ways that artists and scientists work together?

133

Exploring Art

A Museum Just for You

Now that the school year is coming to an end, what are some of the things you can do to continue learning about art? If there is an art museum in your community, or in a place you plan to visit this summer, you have a perfect place to learn more about art.

Most art museums display collections of original artworks in many different **media**, from drawings and paintings to sculpture and **decorative arts**. Some museums specialize in certain types of art, such as the art of a particular country, culture, or time period. Every museum is a valuable educational resource, no matter what the nature of its collections. Perhaps your class can do some research to discover what several of the major museums in this country have in their collections.

You have made many different kinds of art throughout this school year. What are the best artworks you have created? How can you judge this? With your teacher and the rest of the class, set up your own museum exhibit of the best work that you and your classmates created during the school year. Where will your museum be? How will you display your work? Your class will have some decision-making to do before creating a museum exhibit. Have fun, and be sure to give your family and friends a chance to admire your artwork in a "museum" setting.

Review

Using What You Have Learned

Umberto Boccioni was an Italian sculptor and painter in the early twentieth century. He belonged to a group of poets and painters who called themselves **Futurists**. As you can guess from the name, these artists had a great interest in new ideas and the future. They celebrated the motion and energy of the modern world in paintings and sculptures in which everything seemed to be happening at once. *The City Rises* is one of Boccioni's best-known paintings. Study it, applying the knowledge of art you have learned.

Umberto Boccioni, The City Rises. 1910. Oil on canvas. 6'6½" × 9'10½". Collection, The Museum of Modern Art, New York, Mrs. Simon Guggenheim Fund.

1. Did the artist plan a good **composition** for this painting? Describe how your eyes move around the painting.

2. Point out the use of **lines** in the painting. How do these lines add to the overall effect of the work?

3. How did the artist use **color** to express his subject? Name the colors he used. Why are these colors appropriate?

4. How did Boccioni achieve **unity**?

5. How did the artist show **depth** and **distance** in the painting? Does he show **space** realistically?

6. Describe Boccioni's **technique** of painting. What kinds of brushstrokes did he use? What do they express?

7. What is the **theme** of this painting? Did the artist successfully use the **elements** and **principles of design** to communicate his theme? Why or why not?

Glossary

abstract A style of art in which lines, shapes, colors, patterns, and textures are simplified or exaggerated. Geometric shapes and a lack of detail are often features of abstract art.

adornment Any ornament that is added to a person or object as decoration.

advertising art Graphic art that communicates positive messages about a product or idea. Advertising art may be seen on billboards, in magazines and newspapers, and on television.

alternating pattern or **rhythm** A pattern or rhythm in which two or more shapes, designs, or colors repeat in a one-after-the-other sequence.

analogous /ə-nal'-ə-gəs/ **colors** Colors that are closely related because they have one hue in common. For example, blue, blue-violet, and violet all contain the color blue. Analogous colors appear next to one another on the color wheel.

animation /an-ə-mā'-shən/ A type of motion picture made by putting together a series of drawings or photographs in a sequence that shows a gradual, progressive change in movement. When the series of pictures is run together at high speed, the illusion of motion is created.

animator /an'-ə-māt-ər/ One who creates drawings or other artworks to be used in the making of an animated motion picture.

architect /är'-kə-tekt/ A person who designs the inside and outside plan of a building and selects materials to be used for its construction.

architecture /är'-kə-tek-chər/ The art of designing and building structures. All types of buildings, from skyscrapers to churches and houses, are examples of architecture.

armature /är'-mə-chŏŏr/ A skeleton-like framework used to support figures of clay or papier-mâché. An armature keeps a sculpted figure with parts that stick out from drooping or falling apart. Armatures can be made of wire, piping, metal rods, rolled paper, or similar materials.

artist-naturalists Nature artists who study plant and animal life in their natural surroundings and then accurately draw or paint what they have observed. These artists often make valuable contributions to science as well as art.

assemblage /ə-sem'-blij/ A piece of three-dimensional art made by combining a collection of unrelated materials into a new creation. An assemblage can be a free-standing sculpture, a piece mounted on a panel, or even a type of three-dimensional collage.

asymmetrical /ā-sə-me'-tri-kəl/ A type of balance or arrangement in which two sides of a work of art are not exactly alike, yet still appear pleasingly balanced.

background Parts of an artwork that are in the distance and appear behind the objects nearest to the viewer, in the foreground.

balance The arrangement of all parts of an artwork to create a sense of equality on all sides. The weight or size of objects, their placement, and their color must all be balanced in a work of art. Balance is a principle of design.

book jacket The paper "sleeve" that forms the outer covering of a hardcover book.

bound Describes a book with sewn or glued pages attached to an outer cover.

brayer /brā'-ər/ A small, hand-held rubber roller used to spread printing ink evenly over a surface before printing.

brushstroke A line, shape, or texture created by applying paint to a surface with a paintbrush in a particular way.

calligraphic /kal-ə-graf'-ik/ **drawing** A kind of drawing made up of flowing lines and simple, curving shapes much like those used in calligraphy.

calligraphy /kə-lig'-rə-fē/ The art of writing letters and words in a beautiful, ornamental style using pens or brushes.

cartoonist An artist who draws comics—pictures to make people laugh, tell a simple story, or point out problems in society.

carve To create a three-dimensional form by cutting away unwanted parts from a block of wood, stone, or other hard material.

center of interest The most important part of a work of art, to which the viewer's eyes should be immediately drawn. All the other parts of an artwork should center around, be a background for, or draw attention to the center of interest.

cityscape A painting or drawing showing a whole or partial view of a city.

coil A rolled, rope-like shape. Clay coils can be used to create pottery or sculptures.

collage /kə-läzh′/ Artwork created by gluing bits of paper, fabric, scraps, photographs, or other materials to a flat surface.

color The hue, value, and intensity of an object as seen by the human eye.

color wheel A way of showing relationships among colors in the form of a circle. Colors that are next to one another on the color wheel are called analogous colors; colors opposite each other are complementary colors.

comic book A magazine containing a long series of comic panels which tell lengthier stories than can be told in newspaper comic strips.

comic strip One or more cartoon panels which tell a story or show a sequence of action. Comic strips often feature a continuing cast of characters that audiences become used to.

complementary /käm-plə-ment′-ə-rē/ **colors** Colors that are considered opposites because they share no hue in common and contrast with each other.

compose To create, form, or design by purposely putting together or arranging different parts to create a unified whole.

composition The arrangement of elements of art (shape, line, color, value, texture, and space) in an artwork according to principles of design to create a unified, balanced artwork. The term also refers to any work of art.

contemporary /kən-tem′-pə-rer-ē/ Of or representing the present time.

contour A line which represents or describes the outline of a shape or form. In contour drawing, a subject is represented by an unbroken outline with few or no details.

contrast A great difference between two things, showing how they are unlike each other or opposite. For example, smooth and rough, yellow and violet, and light and shadow are all opposites, showing contrasting qualities. Contrasting colors, patterns, shapes, or textures add excitement, variety, and emphasis to a work of art.

contrasting colors Colors that are opposite each other on the color wheel because they share no hues in common; also called complementary colors. Yellow and violet, blue and orange, and red and green are complementary, or contrasting, color pairs. (*See also* complementary colors.)

cool colors The family of related, or analogous, colors ranging from the greens through the blues and violets. Cool colors are so-called because they remind people of cool places, things, and feelings.

crayon etching A type of picture made by coating paper with several layers of wax crayon and then scratching a design into the surface with a sharp object, revealing crayon colors in underneath layers.

crayon resist A type of picture in which wax crayon is used to cover certain areas of a surface that the artist does not want to be affected by paint or another substance to be put over the crayon. Since wax repels water, the paint will not cover the crayoned part.

decoration Any ornament or other feature that is not a necessary part of something yet adds beauty and interest.

decorative arts Such arts as furniture-making, glassblowing, rug and fabric design, and other handicrafts which result in functional objects that have great appeal for their beauty.

depth Distance from front to back, or top to bottom, of an object. A three-dimensional object can be measured in length, width, and depth.

design To plan and arrange all the parts of an artwork. Also, an organized, creative arrangement of the elements of an artwork, such as lines, shapes, textures, spaces, and colors.

diorama /dī-ə-ram'-ə/ A scene, usually in miniature, in which three-dimensional models are displayed against a realistic painted background.

distort To change the way something really looks by twisting it out of its natural form or exaggerating its features.

dominant The part of a design that is most important, powerful, or has the most influence.

elements of design Basic parts that are put together to compose an artwork. These include line, shape, space, texture, color, and value.

emphasis /em'-fə-səs/ The use of sizes, shapes, colors, textures, and other elements and principles of design to draw attention to certain areas or objects in a work of art.

engrave To carve or cut pictures, letters, or designs into a hard material such as wood, metal, or ivory, using sharp tools.

exaggerate To change the way something really looks by making some features larger or more important so that they stand out.

expressive Showing a strong emotion, mood, or feeling so that others can see and identify it.

Fauves (fōhvz) A small group of artists in France in the early 1900s who experimented with using intense colors in unrealistic ways to express personal views and feelings. People named them the Fauves, or "wild beasts."

fibers Natural or man-made threads that make up such materials as string, yarn, and fabric.

flip book An animated sequence in book form, made by drawing a single action on each page and flipping the pages from back to front.

folk art Traditional art made by people who have had no formal art training, and who instead practice art styles and craftsmanship that have been handed down through generations.

foreground Parts of an artwork that appear to be in front, nearest to the viewer.

form The three-dimensional structure of an object. In two dimensions, a form is represented as a shape.

frame A single picture in a series of pictures making up the length of an animated film or other motion picture.

free-form Having an irregular, or nongeometric, shape. A free-form shape is made up of curving, irregular lines.

Futurists A group of artists and writers in Italy from 1909 to 1916 who tried to break ties with the past and instead looked forward to the future. They symbolized the future with artwork that expressed the speed, energy, and motion of the modern age.

geodesic /jē-ə-des'-ik/ **dome** A dome built by joining straight, lightweight bars into connected geometric shapes. These domes were first designed by architect R. Buckminster Fuller.

geometric Based on simple lines and shapes from geometry, such as circles, squares, triangles, rectangles, and the like.

graphic artist or **designer** A person who designs art to be used for commercial purposes, such as advertisements, signs, and book jackets.

handicrafts Crafts such as pottery, baskets, rugs, candles, and dozens of other useful or decorative items that people traditionally make by hand.

hand puppet A type of movable figure that fits over a person's hand and is controlled by moving the fingers.

hieroglyphics /hī-rə-glif'-iks/ A system of writing using pictures rather than words and letters. Usually, the term *hieroglyphics* refers to the ancient writing system of the Egyptians.

horizontal A position parallel to the horizon, or straight across rather than up-and-down. A horizontal line on a piece of paper is parallel to the top and bottom edges of the paper.

Hudson River School A small group of American painters who in 1825 created the first truly American style of painting that focused on the American landscape.

hue /hyü/ The property of a color that makes it appear green, red, yellow, blue, etc., to our eyes. Hue is often used as another word for color.

ideal A representation or symbol of perfection, beauty, excellence, or other valued qualities.

illusion The appearance of something that gives a false impression. An artist can use techniques of perspective to create the illusion of depth on a two-dimensional surface.

illustrator An artist who creates and designs pictures to explain a point, show an important part of a story, or add decoration to a book, magazine, or other printed work.

image A drawing, painting, photograph, sculpture, or other artistic reproduction of a human or other form. An image can also be a mental picture of something that is not present.

in-betweens The middle pictures in a flip book, showing the actions that occur between the first and the last action in a sequence.

intermediate /int-ər-mēd′-ē-ət/ **colors** Colors that are created by mixing a primary color with a secondary color. The resulting hues—red-orange, red-violet, blue-green, etc.—are called intermediate colors.

invent To create something new that has never been seen before, using one's imagination.

landscape A painting or drawing showing a scene from nature, often including mountains, trees, rivers, fields, and other outdoor scenery.

landscape architect A person who designs and arranges plots of land, such as parks, for people to use and enjoy.

layout A plan, design, or arrangement of printed material, such as lettering and artwork, to be used in graphic art.

line A continuous mark with length and direction, created by a point that moves across a surface. A line can vary in length, width, direction, curvature, and even color. Line can be two-dimensional (created by moving a pencil on paper), three-dimensional (created with string or wire), or even implied (not represented by an actual line but suggested by the boundaries of a shape or form). Line can also refer to the outline or shape of an object.

loom A frame or machine used for weaving fibers (yarn, thread, string, jute, etc.) to create cloth. A loom can be small and simple, such as a cardboard loom, or large and complex, like a machine loom in a factory.

Luminists /lü′-mə-nəstz/ A group of nineteenth-century American painters who continued the tradition of painting the American landscape but who started to emphasize the effects of light on the sky and other objects.

main shape The basic geometric or free-form shape that underlies the structure of an object.

marionette /mar-ē-ə-net′/ An advanced form of puppet, usually made of wood, that is operated from above by moving strings attached to its jointed arms, legs, and body.

mat A border or frame for a picture, usually made out of cut-out cardboard or thick paper.

media Any materials, such as paint, colored pencils, charcoal, clay, or papier-mâché, that are used to produce a work of art. Media also refers to the various techniques, such as painting, collage, or sculpture, with which these materials are used. Media is the plural form of *medium.*

medieval /mēd-ē′vəl/ From or of the Middle Ages in Europe, A.D. 500–1500.

medium The material used to create a work of art: oil paints, watercolor, pastel, clay, chalk, etc. Also, the technique, such as painting, sculpture, or drawing, in which a work of art was made. Medium is the singular form of *media.*

memorabilia /mem-ə-rə-bil′-ē-a/ Items saved by people as reminders of the past.

middleground Parts of an artwork that appear to be between objects in the foreground and the background.

model A person or thing used as an example or pattern for an artist to follow when creating a work of art. Also, a small copy or image that represents a larger object. *Model* is also a verb used to describe the act of forming a sculpture by building up or adding on clay, papier-mâché, or another material to create a work of art.

monochrome A color scheme using only one hue and its variations. Also, a work of art limited to such a color scheme.

movement The arrangement of parts of a design to create a sense of motion, causing the viewer's eye to move from one point of emphasis to the next. *Movement* can also refer to a trend or school in art.

negative space The empty space surrounding shapes or forms in a work of art.

neutral colors The colors black, white, brown, and gray are considered neutral, or "non-colorful" colors that aren't found in the rainbow.

oil paint A kind of opaque paint made by mixing colored pigment with a special kind of oil.

opaque /ō-pāk′/ Something that does not let light in and cannot be seen through; the opposite of transparent. (*See also* transparent.)

organic /ȯr-gan′-ik/ Important or essential part of a whole, like part of a living thing.

outline A line that shows or creates the outer edges of a shape or form, also sometimes called the contour. (*See also* contour.)

overlapping Covering part or all of a shape or form with another shape or form.

panel One of a series of boxed pictures in a comic strip or comic book.

papier-mâché /pā-pər-mə-shā′/ An art material made of paper torn into strips or pulp and covered with a paste or glue mixture. It can be molded into different shapes when wet and is solid and very hard when dry.

pattern The repetition, or repeated, regular use, of shapes, lines, colors, or textures in a design.

perspective A technique of representing three-dimensional scenes or objects on a flat, two-dimensional surface.

pictograph /pik′-tə-graf/ Drawn or painted symbols representing things, ideas, or stories. Before alphabets were developed, people communicated using such picture symbols.

pinch method A method of hand-building pottery by pressing, pulling, and pinching a ball of clay into the desired shape.

Pop art A style of art in which everyday, popular images were used as subject matter. Common subject matter in Pop art included comic strips, product packages, and advertising art.

portrait /por′-trət/ A painting, sculpture, drawing, photograph, or other work of art which features a person, group of people, or animal, usually emphasizing the faces.

positive space The lines, shapes, or forms that fill a work of art. Positive space is partly defined by the negative space surrounding it.

potter A person who makes pottery.

potter's wheel A flat, spinning disc on which soft clay is placed and shaped by hand.

primary colors The hues red, yellow, and blue. When mixed in different combinations, these three colors produce all other colors, except white. The primary colors themselves cannot be produced by mixing any other colors together.

primitive art Art made by self-taught artists with little or no training in techniques of art.

principles of design Guidelines that aid artists in arranging and composing designs in the best way. The principles of design include balance, contrast, variety, pattern, rhythm, emphasis, and unity. (*See also* elements of design.)

progressive pattern or **rhythm** A pattern or rhythm that develops step-by-step, as from larger to smaller or smaller to larger.

proportion The relationship of the size or placement of one part to another part or to a whole. In painting and sculpture, for example, an artist tries to show the right relationship, or proportion, of a nose to a face, a head to a body, and so on.

puppeteer /pəp-ə-tir′/ An artist who creates and/or operates puppets.

purpose The intended use for a work of art.

quilt A bedcover made by stitching two layers of fabric together, usually in an ornamental design, and stuffing the layers with padding. Quilts are usually made out of odds and ends of material.

radial /rād′-ē-əl/ **balance** A type of balance in which parts are arranged in a regular pattern around a central point, like spokes coming out from the center of a bicycle wheel.

raised surface Any surface in which a texture or design sticks up from a level background.

realistic The true appearance of people, objects, and scenes as seen by the human eye. Realistic art attempts to re-create the colors, textures, shapes, and arrangements of actual subjects.

relief A type of sculpture that is halfway between solid free-standing sculpture and flat painting. In a relief, figures rise up from a background that is flat or has hollowed-out parts.

Renaissance /ren-ə-sänts′/ A period in European history starting in the fourteenth century and ending in the seventeenth century. This period was marked by a reawakening and growth in the arts and the birth of modern science.

repeating pattern or **rhythm** The use of the same line, shape, color, or texture over and over to form a predictable pattern or rhythm.

rod puppet A form of puppet that is attached to a stick or rod and controlled from below.

rhythm The regular repetition of lines, shapes, colors, or patterns in a work of art.

rubbing An artwork in which a duplicate, or copy, of a textured surface is made by rubbing the edge of a crayon, pastel, or other drawing tool over a piece of paper which rests on the surface.

scale The relationship between the sizes of parts in an artwork to their size in reality. If a picture is drawn to scale, all of its parts are equally smaller or larger than the parts in the original.

score To press a pointed instrument into but not through paper or thin cardboard, creating a line where it will bend easily. In clay work, artists score grooves or scratches into clay edges that are to be joined together.

scrimshaw A folk art in which line drawings are carved, or engraved, into bone or ivory.

sculpt To carve, model, or construct figures or objects in stone, wood, metal, clay or other materials, producing a three-dimensional work of art.

sculpture A carving, model, assemblage, or other created form that has height, width, and depth. Sculpture is three-dimensional art.

secondary color A color created by mixing together two of the three primary colors: red, yellow, and blue. The secondary colors are orange, green, and violet. Orange is a mixture of red and yellow, green is a mixture of yellow and blue, and violet is a mixture of red and blue.

self-portrait A picture of an artist that is drawn, painted, photographed, or sculpted by the artist.

shade A variation of a hue created by adding varying amounts of black to that hue. For example, adding black to red results in a darker shade of red.

shading A technique of showing different values of light and dark in a picture. Shading is a way of making a picture appear more realistic and three-dimensional.

shadow puppet A type of rod puppet that is moved behind a lighted screen so that only the action of the puppet's shadow can be seen. (*See also* rod puppets.)

shape A definite form shown in two dimensions, indicated by lines or a change in color or shading that defines the shape's boundaries. Shapes come in two main types: geometric (squares, circles, triangles, etc.) and free-form (irregular, curving outlines).

silhouette /sil-ə-wet′/ An outline of a solid shape filled in completely, like a shadow, with no inside details.

simplify To make something appear simpler or less complicated by removing details and focusing instead on what is most important about the subject, such as its main shape.

sketch A simple, rough drawing done quickly to catch the chief features and the overall impression of an object or scene.

sketchbook A book or pad of blank drawing paper used by artists to record sketches from life or from the imagination.

slab method A technique of making pottery in which a thick, flat slab, or slice, of clay is cut into shapes which are joined together to form a useful or decorative object.

slip A creamy mixture of clay, vinegar, and water used to bind two pieces of clay together (such as the slabs making up a square vase).

sphere A perfectly round three-dimensional object, such as a ball or globe.

stencil A pattern consisting of a cut-out design used for printing. Paint, crayon, or another medium is pressed or applied over the stencil, filling in the cut-out spaces so that a design comes through onto the paper underneath.

stenciling A method of printmaking using stencils and a coloring medium to create a design or pattern on paper or another surface.

still life A drawing, painting, collage or other artwork that shows an arrangement of nonmoving, nonliving objects, such as fruit, flowers, bottles, books, and other objects of daily life.

style An artistic technique. Style is a means of expression, using materials, design arrangements, methods of working, and choice of subject matter as a way of showing the unique qualities of an individual, culture, or time period.

stylized Designed to show something in a simpler way that represents a pattern or style rather than the way something actually looks.

subtractive sculpture A type of sculpture that has been created by subtracting, or taking away, material from a larger block or piece of material.

sumi-e A kind of Japanese brush drawing done with simple, flowing, curving lines that are created with careful brushstrokes.

symbol A letter, picture, or sign that stands for a real object or idea.

symmetrical /sə-me′-tri-kəl/ A type of balance in which the contents on either side of a center line are exactly the same, like a mirror image.

tab A small flap or tongue of paper cut to fit in a slot in order to connect two pieces of paper.

technique A way of using methods and materials to achieve a desired result.

texture The look and feel of a surface: rough, smooth, silky, and so on.

theme The subject or topic of a work of art.

three-dimensional Having the qualities of length, width, and depth.

tint A variation of a hue created by adding varying amounts of white to that hue. For example, adding white to red results in pink, a tint of red.

title The name given to a painting, drawing, sculpture, or other work of art.

tone The tint, shade, brightness, or value of a color. Adding gray to a color results in a tone of that color.

totem /tōt′-əm/ An object or image that serves as a symbol or emblem of a family, person, idea, or experience.

totem pole A pole or pillar of wood carved and painted with totem images showing the history, traditions, and legends of the Northwest Indians.

transparent Allowing light to pass through so that objects can be seen underneath; the opposite of opaque.

two-dimensional Flat, having only the qualities of length and width.

unify To make all parts in a work of art look as if they belong together in a complete whole.

unity The quality of being whole and complete. A work of art has unity when all of its parts are balanced and organized to achieve harmony.

value The lightness or darkness of tones or colors. For example, white and yellow have a light value, and black and purple have a dark value.

variation A change in form, shape, detail, or appearance that makes an object different from similar objects that it resembles.

variety The use of different or assorted lines, shapes, textures, colors, and other elements of design to create interest in a work of art.

vary To make different in some way by making a change in character or feature.

vertical A line or shape that stands upright, or straight up and down. On a piece of paper, a vertical line is parallel to the side edges of the paper.

viewfinder A small window in a camera or a rectangle cut into a piece of paper that an observer can look through to see what will appear in a photograph or picture taken of that scene.

visualize To form a mental picture using one's imagination and memory.

visual memory The ability to remember what something actually looks like when it is not available for viewing.

warm colors The family of related, or analogous, colors ranging from the reds through the oranges and yellows. Warm colors are so-called because they remind people of warm places, things, and feelings.

warp The vertical, or up-and-down, threads that are first attached to the top and bottom of a loom.

wash A way of applying thin, watery paint to paper with large, sweeping brushstrokes.

watercolors A type of water-based transparent paint. Also, a painting done with watercolors.

weaving Artwork created by lacing together or interlocking fibers, such as strands of thread, yarn, or other materials, on a loom to create a piece of fabric or a decorative work.

weft The fibers that are woven back and forth (horizontally) across the vertical warp fibers to make a solid fabric or woven design.

Artists' Reference

All the works by famous artists presented in this book are listed here. Use this list to locate particular paintings, drawings, sculptures, and other artworks and to find works by artists who especially interest you.

Index

Acknowledgments

We gratefully acknowledge the valuable contributions of the following artists, consultants, editorial advisors, and reviewers who participated in the development of this book: Ruth Jones and C.J. Greenwald, teachers, St. Luke's Lutheran Day School, La Mesa, CA; Mirta Golino, art educator and editorial advisor, San Diego; Jeff Jurich, animator and writer, Celluloid Studios, Denver; Dennis Smith, sculptor, Highland, UT; Virginia Gadzala, costume designer, San Diego; Phyllis Thurston, former Art Supervisor, Pinellas County School District, Clearwater, FL; Judy Chicago and Mary Ross Taylor, Through the Flower, Benicia, CA; Andrew Blanks, Jr., art teacher, Johnston Middle School, Houston; Barbara Pearson Roberts, teacher, Sabal Palm Elementary School, Tallahassee; Shirley and Terry McManus, puppetry consultants, "Puppets Please," San Diego; Dr. Wayne Woodward, associate professor of art education, Georgia Southwestern College; Mary Riggs of Riggs Galleries, San Diego; Anna Ganahl, Director of Public Relations, Art Center College of Design, Pasadena; Françoise Gilot, artist, La Jolla, CA; Leven C. Leatherbury, independent consultant in art education, San Diego; Betty Cavanaugh, curriculum consultant in art education, Upland, CA; Joel Hagen, artist and writer, Oakdale, CA; Kellene Champlin, Art Supervisor, Fulton County Schools, Atlanta; Mar Gwen Land, art teacher, Montgomery Jr. High School, San Diego; LaRene McGregor, fiber artist, McKenzie Bridge, OR; Norma Wilson, former art teacher and editorial advisor, San Diego; Dr. Ann S. Richardson, Supervisor of Art, Foreign Languages, and Gifted and Talented Education, Charles County Public Schools, LaPlata, MD; Talli Larrick, educator and writer, El Cajon, California; Mary Apuli, Coordinator of Elementary Program, Indiana School District No. 16, Minneapolis; Carol Widdop-Sonka, artist and writer, San Diego; Virginia Fitzpatrick, art educator and writer, Bloomington, IN; Evelyn Ackerman, artist, Era Industries, Culver City, CA; Judy Kugel, teacher trainer for Learning to Read Through the Arts, New York City; Arlie Zolynas, educator and author, San Diego; Nancy Remington, Principal, Sacramento Country Day School, Sacramento; Kay Alexander, Art Consultant, Palo Alto School District, Palo Alto, CA; Billie Phillips, Lead Art Supervisor, St. Louis Public Schools, St. Louis; Sister Marie Albert, S.S.J., Principal, St. Callistus School, Philadelphia; Robert Vickrey, artist, Orleans, MA.

We especially appreciate the students from the following schools who contributed the student art reproduced in this series: O.H. Anderson Elem. School, Mahtomedi, MN; Atkinson Elem. School, Barnesville, MN; W.D. Hall Elem. School, El Cajon, CA; Idlewild Elem. School, Memphis, TN; Irving Elem. School, St. Louis, MO: MacArthur Elem. School, Indianapolis, IN; Oakwood Elem. School, Knoxville, TN; John Roe Elem. School, St. Louis, MO; Taylors Falls School District #140, Taylors Falls, MN; Washington Elem. School, Pamona, CA; Enterprise Elem. School, Enterprise, FL; Kellogg Elem. School, Chula Vista, CA; Learning to Read Through the Arts, New York, NY; Lewis School, San Diego; Woodcrest Elem. School, Fridley, MN; Westwood Elem. School, San Diego; Indep. School District #16, Minneapolis, MN; St. Luke's Lutheran Day School, La Mesa, CA; Country Day School, Sacramento, CA; Budd School, Fairmont, MN; Park Terrace Elem. School, Spring Lake Park, MN; Audubon Elem. School, Baton Rouge, LA; Chilowee Elem. School, Knoxville, TN; Logan Elem. School, San Diego; Grassy Creek Elem. School, Indianapolis, IN; Earle Brown Elem. School, Brooklyn Center, MN; Jefferson Elem. School, Winona, MN; Calvert Elem. School, Prince Frederick, MD; Barnsville Elem. School, Barnsville, MN; Ridgedale Elem. School, Knoxville, TN; Children's Creative and Performing Arts Academy, San Diego; Steven V. Correia School, San Diego; Walnut Park Elem. School, St. Louis, MO

Although it is impossible to acknowledge all the contributors to this project, we express special thanks for the generous efforts of the following individuals: Janet Reim, Gail Kozar, Rae Murphy, Jan Thompson, Gerald Williams, Timothy Asfazadour, Judy Cannon, Helen Negley, Crystal Thorson, Rachelle and Tyler Bruford, Mary Bluhm, David Zielinski, David Oliver, Daniel and Carl Bohman, Anne G. Allen, Bao Vuong, Gail W. Guth, Signe Ringbloom, Claire Murphy, Joan Blaine, Patrice M. Sparks, and Larke Johnston.

Coronado Staff: Marsha Barrett Lippincott, Level 1 Editor; Janet Kylstad Coulon, Level 2 Editor; Deanne Kells Cordell, Level 3 Editor; Carol Spirkoff Prime, Level 4 Editor; Patricia McCambridge, Level 5 Editor; DeLynn Decker, Level 6 Editor; Janis Heppell, Project Designer; Lisa Peters, Designer; Myrtali Anagnostopoulos, Designer; Debra Saleny, Photo Research.